CONNECTION

CONNECTION

Hollywood Storytelling meets Critical Thinking

RANDY OLSON   DORIE BARTON   BRIAN PALERMO

Prairie Starfish Productions

Connection
Hollywood Storytelling Meets Critical Thinking
Randy Olson, Dorie Barton, Brian Palermo

Copyright © 2013 by Prairie Starfish Productions

September 2013

Prairie Starfish Productions
5254 Melrose Ave. #D-112
Los Angeles, CA 90038
www.cnxnstory.com

Cover and interior design by Vanessa Maynard
Edited by Debra Almgren-Horwitz

LCCN: 2013915698
ISBN-978-0615872384 (Print)

Printed in the United States of America

TABLE OF CONTENTS

PRAISE FOR "CONNECTION"

"We want people to take what we say to heart AND a story does it best, BUT most of us don't know how to turn our thoughts into stories, THEREFORE most of us need to read this book."
— *Alan Alda, Actor, Writer*

"Based on their extraordinary narratives, Randy, Dorie and Brian have combined and sculpted *Connection* into an amazing resource for anyone with a story to tell (even scientists!)."
— *Ron Britton, Wildlife Biologist, U.S. Fish and Wildlife Service*

"*Connection* provides a series of clear and descriptive formulas for telling good stories, while still appreciating that storytelling is an art. It's a must-read for anyone interested in being understood."
— *Jennifer Jacquet, Assistant Professor of Environmental Studies, New York University*

"Storytelling is meant to connect a message to a person's heart, mind and belief system, thus inviting one to take action or make a change in their life. *Connection* provides a road map to do just that."
— *Jeff King, Author of "Beyond Drama"*

"We sponsored the very first version of the *Connection* workshop which for us was both eye-opening and heart opening. Randy, Dorie and Brian helped us think about the stories we want to tell, and to speak from our feelings as well as from our intellects. This is so important, yet rarely talked about by scientists and bureaucrats (like me!). I overcame a shyness about expressing my passion for my work and was able to really communicate the story of what I do and why. This book now takes their teachings even further in thinking deeply about stories and how to tell them effectively."
— *Shelley Luce, Santa Monica Bay Restoration Commission and Foundation*

"A great guide to bridging the gut/data & art/science divide."
— *Andrew Revkin, NY Times, Dot Earth Blog*

"Two years ago, when I hosted the *Connection* Storytelling Workshop at NRDC, I got to see sides of my co-workers I never knew existed. As Randy, Dorie and Brian guided us through intensive story development exercises and wildly entertaining improv games, we all saw our work—and learned how to talk about it—through a new, more human, even heroic, lens. Now the book captures the essence of what we experienced, providing just the right combination of explanation, instruction and encouragement. If you are serious about becoming a more effective communicator, read *Connection*. No matter who you are or what you do, this book will help you uncover your inner storyteller and the treasure trove of stories you have to tell."
— *Tina Swanson, Natural Resources Defense Council*

THE MAKING OF STORIES

"A story begins when something happens." — Randy Olson

"It's all the same story." — Dorie Barton

"Make your story relatable." — Brian Palermo

Because this book is about the power of simplicity in broad communication, we begin with these three individual statements. We, of course, have a lot more to say than just this. But if each of us had to choose just one thing for you to take away, these would be our simple messages.

INTRODUCTION

by Randy Olson

Hollywood has gone flat. You see it everywhere today. And by "flat" I don't mean like a can of Coke that's been left out. I mean in the sense of Thomas Friedman's book, *The World Is Flat*. He refers to the way the playing field of the planet has been leveled by the internet and modern commerce. The same thing has happened with Hollywood.

There used to be a whole Hollywood way of life of fast talking, fast living, and fast job changes. You can read about it in books from the 1980s and 90s. Oscar-winning producer Julia Phillips painted a perfect portrait of that lifestyle with her autobiography, *You'll Never Eat Lunch in This Town Again*. Hollywood used to be such a different, crazy, and alien place. But then the internet and other technology came along, and things went flat.

Suddenly, people in Peoria, Illinois were building websites, shooting videos, doing lunches, creating productions, and ending up with the same fast pace as Hollywood. People living in the rarefied air of the Hollywood Hills were brought down in stature to the same level as the folks in Shawnee, Kansas. In the sense of Friedman, relative to the rest of society, Hollywood went flat.

We open with that as our basic premise. Today everyone is Hollywood. So why not make use of the same tools for mass communication perfected in the movie business over the past century, even though you don't live anywhere near Tinseltown.

THE STORYTELLING CONNECTION

This book is about telling stories. It's about *you* telling stories, *me* telling stories, *your neighbor* telling stories, *the President* telling stories—everyone telling stories.

Why are we all telling stories? Because they are a fundamental part of communication, and because they can be a powerful
part of persuasion. It is our nature, as Nancy Duarte explained
in *Resonate* and Jonathan Gottschall took further in *The Storytelling Animal.*

From the lawyer in Alliance, Nebraska, to the travel agent in
Owensboro, Kentucky, to the public health worker in Mesa,
Arizona—everyone has a need to tell stories. The lawyer tells
stories to persuade a jury, the travel agent tells stories to vaca-
tioners to get them excited about a destination, and the public
health worker tells stories to patients to warn them of risky
behavior. They all need to tell stories.

This is what we are here to help with—to make this "connection" between the non-Hollywood and Hollywood in a way
that goes beyond the glitter, noise, and nonsense. We're interested in helping you, the reader, bring the power of storytelling
to your daily life. The way we do this is not just by raving about
the joys and power of storytelling, but by getting down to how
you do it—specifically by using a set of templates we're going
to introduce.

The content of what we offer arises primarily from a workshop we organized following the publication of my first book,
Don't Be Such a Scientist: Talking Substance in an Age of Style. I left
a career as a scientist and ventured to Hollywood in an effort to
better understand the basic principles of mass communication.
With that book, I was reporting back to the science world what
I had learned.

To implement my message, I recruited two Hollywood pro-
fessionals, Dorie Barton and Brian Palermo, as co-instructors
in what came to be known as our "Connection Storymaking

Workshop." Over the past three years we conducted it with a number of organizations, including the National Park Service, the Natural Resources Defense Council, the U.S. Fish and Wildlife Service, and the Association for the Sciences of Limnology and Oceanography.

Out of those experiences we advanced our knowledge of storytelling and eventually worked our way down to one simple storytelling tool that we call the "WSP Model," which stands for Word, Sentence, Paragraph.

Our overall message is not complicated. So many people have big stories to tell but are lost in the details and complexities. We have developed this simple process to shrink down your story at the start so you know what it is you're trying to say. Then through elements of improv training, you can make your story more human and "relatable" to the general audience.

That's pretty much it. Yes, we're going to draw it out for an entire book because there's a lot of associated information for you to know; plus, we have many important (and fun) stories we want to tell you. Furthermore, our workshop is really entertaining, so we've done our best to write this book in a way that gives you the feeling you're experiencing the workshop yourself. We hope that by the end of this book you'll feel at least a little bit like you spent the day with us, living and breathing storytelling.

There's a lot to the telling of stories, but in the end, we mostly just want to keep things as simple as possible. That's crucial in today's world. It's the reason Twitter was created. Simplicity is the ultimate sophistication and no longer just an option – it is essential to survival. That's what we're here to help you with.

RANDY OLSON

RANDY OLSON is the writer/director of the feature films *Flock of Dodos: The Evolution-Intelligent Design Circus*, (Tribeca '06, Showtime '07), *Sizzle: A Global Warming Comedy* (Outfest '08), and author of *Don't Be Such a Scientist: Talking Substance in an Age of Style* (Island Press '09). His work focuses on the challenges involved in communicating science to the general public and on the current attacks on mainstream science in fields such as evolution and climate science. He is a former marine biologist (Ph.D. Harvard University) who achieved tenure at the University of New Hampshire before changing careers to filmmaking by obtaining an M.F.A. in Cinema from the University of Southern California. He is an adjunct faculty member with the Wrigley Institute for Environmental Studies at USC. His production company, Prairie Starfish Productions, is based at Raleigh Studios in Los Angeles.

1. OVERVIEW: ROUGHING IT

1. ONCE UPON A STORYTELLING WORKSHOP

Hi, everybody. Welcome to our workshop! Glad you could join us. I've got a couple of great co-instructors here with me—Dorie and Brian. I'll introduce them in detail shortly, but for starters, we have one simple message for you...

YOU CAN ALL BE GREAT STORYTELLERS!

That's our opening premise. And it's true. I was once a pretty lousy storyteller. Just ask my mother. She says that when I was five, I used to watch television shows, then regurgitate their contents to her. While she was doing the house cleaning, I would go on and on, following her from one room to the next, telling her about the show I had just watched, not really knowing myself what the point of the story was.

I've gotten better. I promise. And if I can get better, so can you.

We have a lot of work ahead of us. We hope you will make the "connection" with what we have to say.

What we mean by "connection" is the idea of separate minds coming together to enlighten each other in new ways. When we put the workshop together we just sort of thought we'd teach a bunch of stuff separately. It never occurred to us the extent to which we would end up learning so much from each other because of our three different backgrounds. I think you'll sense this as you read along.

One aspect of our level of connection is our continuous references to each other's sections. This is not a contrivance. We really have taught each other a great deal and hit these "connection moments" repeatedly as we've gotten to know our own material better through each other's insights.

The bulk of the book is our three individual sections, and I'll just give you a simple warning of how they are going to read. You'll find my material to be a bit like broccoli and Brussels sprouts. Dorie's section is more like a fine meal at a chic Hollywood (of course) restaurant. And Brian... well, his part is kind of like an ice cream sundae with a shot of Jack Daniels in the center and peyote buttons sprinkled on top.

And not coincidentally, this is actually the way the workshop ends up playing to participants. Dorie and I like to say that she is the single mom, I'm the critical stepfather, and Brian is the absentee father who gets to show up and shower happiness on the kids, then clear out before the going gets tough.

He teaches improv, which is HUGE fun. Dorie and I do fun things in our sections, too, but how are you going to compete with improv? Especially from a member of the world-famous Groundlings Comedy Theater in Hollywood. Plus, Brian is a wild man when he teaches, and he's captured at least a little bit of that lunacy in his section.

We hope you'll find the book as much fun to read as it was for us to write. This stuff is really interesting and really important. And since it is all about storytelling, it makes sense that I should start with a story. So here we go...

A LONG AND DUSTY ROAD

On a chilly Saturday morning in October of 1993, I walked into a classroom at the University of New Hampshire to take a test. I was on the verge of receiving tenure as a professor of marine biology, which would mean guaranteed employment for life. But this test had nothing to do with that.

I sat down at one of the classroom desks and was handed a copy of the GRE, or Graduate Records Exam, which was required for me to apply for a master's degree. Even though I already had a PhD in Biology from Harvard University, I was going back to college. At age thirty-eight.

As I looked at the exam booklet, I smiled. It hadn't changed in appearance since I took it sixteen years earlier when I was applying to graduate school in biology. But then I turned to the seat next to me and saw a young undergraduate woman who had been in the introductory biology course I taught a couple of years earlier. She was staring at me with a wrinkled brow. She said, "Dude... I know why I'm here, but... why are *you* here?"

The next month, I opened the door of my office one afternoon, called to a group of graduate students in the hall to come in, then pointed to my bookshelf that held twenty years of my most prized marine biology books. I said to them, "Take whatever you want—take them all." It was official. I had been accepted to film school at the University of Southern California. Despite receiving tenure, it was time to head a new direction in life.

A month later I was driving the southern route across the United States to Los Angeles. This may sound a little sappy, but honest to goodness, as I drove down through Oklahoma, then across West Texas, I sang to myself, over and over again, Tom Paxton's old travelers song: "It's a long and dusty road, it's a hot and heavy load, and the people that I meet aren't always kind. Some are bad, some are good, some have done the best they could, some have tried to ease my troubled mind. But I can't help but wonder where I'm bound." Which was the truth.

Kinda. Except it kinda wasn't. Because I knew exactly where I was headed—to Hollywood. And I knew exactly what I was headed there to do, which was to figure out the Hollywood system for myself. I wanted to learn why I could teach a course in marine biology and say that giant clams don't live in the ocean more than a couple hundred meters depth, yet Hollywood could make a movie showing them two miles down and my students were more likely to believe the crazy movie than me.

What was it about movies? How was it that when I was young, dinosaurs were just a routine part of being a kid, about as popular as Saturday morning cartoons, then suddenly with *Jurassic Park* in 1993, they became a national obsession. How did it all work, and why did stories—especially those concocted in Hollywood—end up being more powerful than facts?

In my first year as a biology professor, prompted by this growing fascination, I took a course in screenwriting at the Boston Film and Video Foundation. It was a hugely popular intensive two-day workshop, taught by the hugely popular Christopher Keane (whom I would track down twenty years later to co-teach a storytelling workshop). I walked into that course with the blankest of a blank slate for a brain when it came to Hollywood and moviemaking.

It's hard to fathom this in today's world, where almost everybody is now making their own movies, but I was so naive that I did not know how a movie was made. I did not know there was a director. I did not know there was a writer. I just watched movies and enjoyed them and never thought any more analytically about them than you might think about what's inside the digital clock on your bedside table. They just "were."

So I sat down in that Saturday morning lecture with 200 moviemaking wannabes, having paid my $200 dollars, and said to myself that if I find this stuff alien and confusing after an hour, I'm just going to walk out. But then Chris Keane began by showing the opening of the movie *Witness*, with Harrison Ford. And my first thought was, "Hey, I know that movie, I've seen it." So for at least the first five minutes I knew I wouldn't be lost.

And then he started talking about how the movie began—the power and symbolism of the visuals, how little dialogue was used, the selection of the camera angles, and lots of other stuff that I found myself completely understanding. This wasn't a foreign language. This wasn't like the "divs, grads, and curls" of the vector calculus class that I tried to take at Harvard and only made it through two lectures. This was stuff that even people outside of Hollywood could understand.

Then he started talking about basic story structure—about three-act structure—and I was mesmerized. As an undergraduate, I had taken classes in English literature—I guess—though today I could not recall one detail from those classes. What Chris was saying was completely new to me. I knew what the word "story" was, but I never knew there was some sort of structure to a story. I knew nothing of there being three acts to a basic story, which are simply the beginning, the middle, and the end.

It was amazing. Like he was pulling back the curtain on the Great Oz, revealing the people at work behind the giant movie screens of America. After an hour into his lecture I thought, "Wow, he's talking pure Hollywood; I have zero background in this stuff, yet I'm able to understand everything he's saying."

And I think that's where my whole interest, fascination, and connection with Hollywood began. I realized that although it was a far, distant and rumored-to-be-crazy place, the Hollywood people still seem to work on stuff that's easily understood.

It's nearly a quarter century later. It's been a wild, fun, and fantastic journey. And if I had to summarize what the entire journey has been about in a single word (as we will be doing soon for many things), that word would be "story." Stories and storytelling are at the heart of not just Hollywood, but human existence in general—they are everywhere.

And to thoroughly convince you of the importance of stories and storytelling, I take you now to the President of the United States for a word on the need to tell stories. Always.

ONCE UPON A TIME THERE WAS A NON-STORYTELLING PRESIDENT...

A nd that President told Charlie Rose of CBS News in July of 2012 that the greatest shortcoming of his first term was, "my failure to tell a story to the American people." What he meant was that although he did a great job of communicating before he was elected, with slogans like "Yes We Can" and "Change You Can Believe In," he kind of lost his edge.

In the beginning everybody was right there with him. But once he got into office, his followers lost focus. Which is what happens when you fail to tell good stories, because focus is one of the key things that stories provide.

In fact, focus is a lot of what this book is about. It is an increasingly elusive resource in today's noisy, hyper-communicating world. In, *The Writer's Journey*, Christopher Vogler tells of how working on movies drove him to realize, "that focused attention is one of the rarest things in the world."

This is one of the true powers of storytelling—creating focus. Stories are great at the start of a talk when you want to get everyone focused on what you have to say. Or at the start of a book. Like this one.

So let me tell you how this President, despite being "story challenged" in his first term, may have had his re-election saved by a story. Which is rather ironic.

It came in the form of an election campaign commercial. Many of you may recall it. The commercial was produced by the super PAC *Priorities USA* and featured a factory worker in Ohio named Mike Earnest (how's that for a "you can't make this stuff up" last name—in fact, there's a word for this—an "aptronym"—look it up—a name that is aptly suited to its owner).

He told a simple story that even began with, "Out of the blue one day ..." Which is the same sort of opening clause as, "Once upon a time," signaling, "we're headed into a story here."

He says that they were told to build a thirty-foot stage. Then a few days later, "A group of people walked out on that stage and told us the plant is now closed and all of you are fired."

And he finishes by saying, "Mitt Romney made over one hundred million dollars by shutting down our plant and devastated our lives. Turns out when we built that stage it was like building my own coffin, and it just made me sick."

A few days after Obama's victory, *New Yorker* writer Jane Mayer pointed out that the commercial (built around a story) might well have been the deciding factor in the election. She said, "They did some internal studies on this ad which showed that in places where the ad showed, the trustworthiness of Romney was eleven points behind that of Obama. In places where it didn't show, Romney was just five points behind." Most importantly, the places it aired were in borderline regions of the ultimate battleground state, Ohio.

Why did it work so well? It told a good story. It wasn't a recitation of poll numbers and demographic research. It told a story that was simple, clear, compelling, and it came from a voice that was both trustworthy and likeable. Not that anybody necessarily did a background check on Mike Earnest; he just had the look and the accent of a salt-of-the-earth, working class, kind of guy who seemed to be speaking from the depths of his heart when he said that Mitt Romney gave him the shaft. It worked.

So there's your power of storytelling in today's world, plain and simple—still powerful enough to get a President elected. In our frantic, hectic, Twitter-fied, Facebooked, short-attention-span world, a good story still has the ability to cut through everything. And by the way, have you perchance noticed people everywhere these days talking about "the narrative"? It ranges from Jon Stewart asking Obama whether he buys into "the Democratic Party narrative" to virtually every organization sooner or later saying to themselves, "we need to figure out our narrative."

That's storytelling at work in your daily life. And that's why the contents of this book are of value to everyone. The power of story continues, unabated. You just need to learn how to use stories for yourself.

THE PUSHBACK ON STORY STRUCTURE

We are keen on the importance of structure in the telling of stories, but before we get going, let me address what inevitably happens when some people are confronted with this approach. For some, the idea of stories being anything but free-form expression, spontaneously emerging from the gut and the heart, is repulsive. Which is fine. But sometimes there exist patterns in the world that you just can't ignore, and this is one of those times. Let me get a little more analytical about this.

At the core of what we are presenting to you are two forces—the intuitive versus the cerebral. I will refer back to these forces repeatedly. Whenever you start to talk about the idea of any systematic structure to stories, you get people groaning at the idea of "Hollywood formula." What they are resisting is the cerebral side of storytelling—the idea that there exists structure and rules, or constraints, on how a story is told in order to be effective.

This is addressed in the preface of the third edition of Vogler's *The Writer's Journey*. He talks about attacks on "the hero's journey," which is the age-old story of the one individual setting out to combat an opposing force. This is at the core of Hollywood storytelling, as you'll soon learn in Dorie's section. He addresses everything from concerns about "cultural imperialism" to gender bias.

Vogler was one of the pioneers in spotting the structure of stories by adapting the knowledge of Joseph Campbell (who first identified "the monomyth" in storytelling) and Carl Jung (who along with Sigmund Freud pretty much founded modern psychology) into the movies. He produced an internal memo at Disney about the theory behind effective storytelling, which eventually became so widely circulated that he turned it into his hugely popular book. But as a result of blazing that trail, he has also been somewhat of a lightning rod for the pushback.

He concedes that many artists bristle at the notion of there being any standardized patterns to their creativity. And he validates many of the concerns. But in the end, you really can't deny the patterns. After a while, they are just too obvious. Let me put it in terms of my own perspective from having entered into the world of Hollywood after a full career in a completely different—and somewhat opposite—profession.

I JUST TELL STORIES

I was a scientist for many years, then I changed careers by going through film school at the University of Southern California. I took numerous writing courses, was in writers groups, and was exposed to all the standardized ways Hollywood tells stories. One of my all-time favorite moments was when screenwriter Jeff Maguire, who wrote the screenplay for the 1993 Clint Eastwood movie *In the Line of Fire*, spoke to us in film school. In the Q&A, one of the students asked him a very specific and technical question along the lines of how many scenes and beats he preferred to use in the latter part of the second act of his screenplays.

He stared at the student blankly and said something to the effect of, "I have no idea what you are talking about." He went on to say he didn't use books on how to write screenplays. The only thing he did was sit down and tell a good story on paper. Which was awesome to hear. And in terms of going with gut instinct rather than rule books, was comparable to the famous quote from legendary director John Huston (which I've heard first hand from his son, actor Danny Huston) who, when asked by a film student in a similar session for his tips on how to create better characters in his writing replied, "Go to down to Mexico and f*** some whores."

FROM GUT TO HEAD: A SHIFT IN PERSPECTIVE

In Hollywood, it is truly off-putting to listen to vacuous droids running around with their rule books on how stories HAVE to be told. And at a deeper level, as a former scientist who was trained in the inductivist approach to studying nature (the idea of going out into nature with no preconceptions) versus the hypothetico-deductive approach (you might as well have a few ideas in your head on how nature works before you go out and waste your time), I have a slight tendency to be dismissive of the idea that there are constraints on how a story must be told in order to be effective.

But the strange truth for me is that I began my journey into the world of storytelling structure in the fall of 1989 while still a professor of biology with zero background in anything to do with storytelling. As the years go by and I continue to gather more experience, I have found myself slowly moving from the pure intuition "I don't want to cloud my perspective" orientation, to the gradual realization and acceptance that Campbell and Jung really did know what they were talking about. And these days I get to actually see it in action in our workshops.

As we move along, I'm going to tell you about a few specific moments where we feel like we are some sort of storytelling faith healers when we see participants in our workshop undergo the magical transition. We see them start the day with a story that is confusing, ambling, and not at all compelling, but by the end of the workshop they are heading home with a story that is fun, interesting, engaging, and best of all, inspiring.

You can honestly feel a shift in self-esteem. It really does make you feel like a better person to be able to answer the question, "What do you do for a living?" with a story that fascinates people, instead of a ramble that ends with, "... um ... that kinda thing, you know."

We've seen the transitions happen enough now that we are compelled to write this book. And we're feeling brave enough to go out and face the slings and arrows of the same sort that Vogler has clearly endured. In fact, the nice thing is that the whole syndrome was recently captured by Hollywood for a completely different profession—baseball. So let me tell you a little story about this...

WE ARE THE "MONEYBALLERS" OF STORYTELLING

Once upon a time, it was 1971 and I was a junior in high school in Kansas City, Kansas. An hour away was the city of Lawrence, the mystical home of the University of Kansas, where we dreamed of going someday.

In Lawrence was a bar called "The Ball Park," where my best friend, Dave, and I discovered they would not only let us drink beers at age sixteen, they also featured a homegrown, very statistics-oriented game called Ball Park Baseball, where on paper you could play any two World Series teams from 1919 onward.

You could figure out if the 1927 Yankees with the Babe could have beaten the 1963 Yankees with Maris and Mantle. It was an awesome place and an awesome game that had been developed by a professor at the University of Kansas back in the fifties. They also made awesome German potato salad that they served with their ballpark hotdogs. We whiled away countless afternoons and evenings there.

One of the most avid players at the bar was a guy named Bill James, from Holton, Kansas, who went on to develop something called sabermetrics, which today is the guiding light of baseball strategists. He was mentioned in the movie *Moneyball*. So that's the story of my microscopic connection to the movie *Moneyball*, but more importantly, let's consider what that movie was about.

It was about a profession that was traditionally dominated by a visceral/intuitive approach to almost everything. For generations, talent scouts chose up-and-coming players based on their gut feelings about whether a guy had the look and style of a winner. They used player's statistics to identify the exceptional players, but when it came to the finer scale decisions of exactly who to recruit, that was left entirely to the mysticism of the gut—as in, "that kid just looks like a star, I got a good feeling, let's sign him."

Into that scene in the late nineties came Billy Beane (a.k.a. Brad Pitt in the movie), general manager of the Oakland Athletics, who suddenly chose to go with a completely cerebral, analytical, numbers-oriented approach of a sort that no one had ever seen. As in, "the numbers show that tall, lanky kid gets on base 48 percent of the time when there's two outs in the late innings. The numbers say, 'Let's sign him.'"

The result was predictable—major resistance from all the old hands who were married to the gut approach, as was dramatized so perfectly in the movie by the grumpy manager played by Phillip Seymour Hoffman. But the big shock ended up being the 2002 season where the A's, despite having the third lowest salary level, set the consecutive wins record and made it to the playoffs (and again in 2003). All of which ended up being a truly great movie about the head/gut (cerebral/visceral) divide.

So just as there is an element of science to baseball, the same is true of stories, as we can see in movies. It's not a coincidence that the recent Oscar-winning movie *Zero Dark Thirty* was basically the same story as *Legally Blonde II*. (Seriously, Chris Kelly, in the Huffington Post, said about the movie, "I'm not saying these things didn't happen. I'm just saying they also happened in *Legally Blonde II*.") They told the same basic story. That's part of the structural science of storytelling.

Most people know the idea of "formulaic Hollywood storytelling," but they really haven't ever given thought to the fact that the reason the crazy story they tell about "the time the wife locked the keys in the trunk of the car" that *always* makes everyone in the room laugh, is because it has the same sort of perfect narrative structure as a good movie. But it does. And that's why it works.

It all begins by taking a more critical look at the telling of stories. Not just stories up on the screen. All stories. Even about the leaky faucet in your kitchen sink that blew a gasket during your dinner party. They all have structure. So let's look more analytically at storytelling ... just like the Moneyballers.

THE TWO AXES OF STORYTELLING

Axis, singular. Axes, plural. Everybody clear on that? If not, Brian will have some comforting words for you later.

Storytelling is sooooo old. It's a little daunting to even write a book about it. Wouldn't you think everything that could be taught about story-

telling is already in the books? Actually, no—because this book is written for a world that has never existed before. There's never been a generation raised on clicking and texting and tweeting. Never.

Which means all that is old is old. We need new. We need fresh ways to look at things like storytelling. Which means some of what we're presenting is a little new, and a lot of what we're presenting is the same old stuff just a little newer.

So let me start with my own simple formulation of breaking the entire process down into what I call the two axes of story development: the horizontal axis and the vertical axis.

They pretty much match the traditional components of story structure and character. But this is a simpler, more intuitive, more mechanistic way to break down stories. We want your story to be tight and concise—made up of the bare minimum of parts—where nothing is wasted. This refers to the horizontal axis of telling a story over time. And we want it to be alive, human, vibrant, and able to reach into the souls of other humans—coming down from your head, into the heart and gut–thus the vertical axis. The two axes are your pathway to effective storytelling.

Here's how we do it in our workshop. You tell us a story, then together with Dorie and Brian, we help you tighten it up by subjecting it to these two simple axes. The horizontal axis is Dorie's expertise—narrative structure. The vertical axis is Brian's area, improv. Let's take a closer look at each axis.

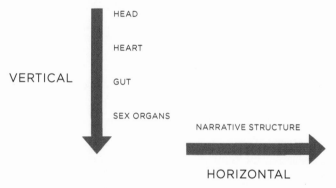

Figure 1. The Two Axes Of Storytelling. Horizontal: Narrative structure. Vertical: Humanizing the story.

THE HORIZONTAL AXIS: NARRATIVE STRUCTURE

This is where Dorie Barton comes in as the voice of expertise on narrative structure. I met her a decade ago and knew her from her outstanding acting skills acquired in her training at the prestigious California Institute of the Arts. I knew she had appeared in movies such as *Meet the Fockers* and *Bewitched* and in lots of great plays. What I didn't know at first was the depth of her background in dramatic writing. But I did mention to her that a friend with a movie company was looking for a script analyst. I recommended her to my friend, they hired her, and I thought little of it, until a year later when my friend said to me, "Do you realize Dorie is the best script analyst we've ever had work for us?"

Cut to a year later when she looked at a draft of a documentary feature I was making and fixed a whole string of story problems with impressive ease. Then cut to a couple years later when it came time for me to create a workshop based around my book. She was the obvious choice.

THE VERTICAL AXIS: HUMANIZING STORIES

This is Brian's area of expertise. The vertical axis was the core message of my first book. When I titled it *Don't Be Such a Scientist*, what I was referring to was the basic piece of advice for scientists to be less analytical and robotic, descending vertically by "coming down out of their heads."

My perspective on the vertical axis originated with the crazy but brilliant acting teacher I had when I first moved to Hollywood. She would scream at us night after night her one core principle of acting. She would say that when an actor wants to reach everyone in the audience—every non-technical, disinterested member of the crowd—there are four organs to draw on: the head (the home of information), the heart (where emotion and passion reside), the gut (the source of humor and intuition), and even at times, if you're "endowed" with enough sex appeal, the sex organs. The object is to move the process down out of your head into these "lower organs."

This is pretty much *the* crucial principle for broad communication. Which makes me think of a minor faux pas I committed a couple of years ago in Norway in addressing this point.

Apparently, in Scandinavia there is an unwritten rule of etiquette about panel discussions, which is that you don't disagree with your fellow panelists. If you want to disagree, that's called "a debate," and meant to be a separate event. Panel discussions, in contrast, are intended to present a unified front of mutually supporting opinions.

So we got to the end of a panel discussion in front of 400 Nordic Communicators of Science, and the moderator asked us to finish with a final statement. When it got to me, I raved about how my fellow panelists were so wonderful, but I ended with, "just one teeny, tiny little thing—I do have to disagree with my colleague here next to me on one minor point."

Well, I glanced at him, then looked up at 400 dropped jaws and 800 wide eyes. I had no clue it was such a transgression. But I could sense it. And at the reception later several people filled me in, all with good humor and smiles, they explained that it just doesn't happen on panels in Scandinavia.

What I disagreed about was his statement that, "I think sometimes, as communicators, we just have to admit there are some topics so trivial, so tedious, so obscure (like the Higgs boson particle maybe?) that we have to concede there is no human way the general public can be made to take an interest."

Which is something I disagree with. As follows.

A HIPPOCRATIC OATH OF COMMUNICATION

I propose a sort of Hippocratic Oath for anyone wanting to communicate anything to anyone. Doesn't matter if you're an action figure memorabilia collector, an obsessive Weather Channel watcher, or antique furniture restoration artist. You have to believe there exists a way to get completely disinterested people interested in what floats your boat.

Physicians swear to "First do no harm." With communications you should swear, "Nothing is impossible to communicate." And even add to that, "I just may not be good enough to do the job, but I shouldn't just give up and call it hopeless."

It's an untestable premise, but let me say this about the four organs. Let's say there's a symposium going on about "Infrastructure Financing in Eastern European Nations." Two guys from building maintenance are sent into the lecture theater to repair a light fixture in the back. They couldn't be more disinterested in what the speaker on stage is saying to one hundred policy wonks in the audience. But then the speaker puts a photo of a gorgeous naked woman up on the screen. Whoa! Suddenly, the two guys stop the repair job for a moment, say to each other, "hold the phone—what's this about?" and listen intently. Suddenly—for some reason—they're interested in Eastern European finance.

Figure 2. *The Sweet Spot. The Greeks knew the head was too informational to reach all the masses, while the sex organs are too crazy. It's in the middle where the heart and the gut reside that the broad audience connects, and thus, the masks of comedy and tragedy.*

The point is that every person has some channel of communication through which they can be reached. It's just a question of how far down the vertical axis you descend. Of course, when you further consider "the lower organs," you come to realize the Greeks, more than a couple thousand years ago, figured out that there is basically this "sweet spot" for broad communication, which means the heart and the gut.

The head gets too dry for non-intellectuals; the sex organs get too crazy for the mainstream. And thus, you realize the two masks of Greek theater—the smiling and frowning masks, comedy and tragedy—were their realization of the true power of broad communication using mostly humor and emotion. So how are you going to get there?

This is where Brian Palermo comes in. He's an accomplished actor. If you saw the movie *The Social Network*, he was the computer science professor. You may have also seen him in many of Jay Leno's "Tonight Show" comic skits. And in lots of TV shows and other movies. But more importantly, he's a longtime member of the world-famous Groundlings Improv Comedy Theater. The Groundlings has been the training ground for some of the most famous comedians of the past few decades—from Will Ferrell and Kristen Wiig, all the way back to Phil Hartman and PeeWee Herman. And not only is he a Groundling, he's also a long time improv instructor.

In fact, since moving to Hollywood, I have worked with more than twenty of the Groundlings. I have cast them in my films and hired them to run the improv segments of my workshops. They are all great and have incredible energy. But the first time I watched Brian run the improv segment of a workshop, I really couldn't believe the guy. He basically took the process to "eleven."

One moment, I was in the corner quietly organizing papers as he was getting started with the improv exercises; the next moment, he's running around in circles, shouting instructions at the poor participants—a group of rather thinky conservation biologists—as they are screaming and crying with laughter, trying to perform the game, "Bunny, Bunny, Bunny" where they are all giant bunnies and—oh, you don't need to know how it works right now, just take it from me, the guy is a force of nature as an instructor.

Improv acting is like one of those animated films that plays at two levels, where the kids don't pick up on the cryptic jokes for the adults. At a superficial level, improv seems to be just a bunch of silly games that are great as icebreakers to get people more relaxed and have fun. But there's a second level to it that is much deeper and even serious.

It's this deeper level that causes corporations to spend lots of money to bring in teams of improv instructors to work with their executives, running them through basic improv exercises. Why would they do such a seemingly silly thing?

The simple answer is, " to get people out of their heads." It's the same thing as taking a walk—getting outside to relax and get a fresher, broader perspective on things. A day of improv exercises is like taking a whole bunch of walks in a row. It's all about the vertical axis. It brings you down out of your head, into the lower organs with humor and emotion, making you more of a human. And that's what the general public likes— human beings.

So keeping in mind the need for stories to be well structured yet also human, let's get started on how to enter into "story mode" and learn why it's so powerful.

2. STARTING A STORY

FOOTBALL GAMES AS ICONIC STORIES

Time to get started on the basics of building a story. Our long-term goal is for you to develop "story sense." What that means is that you eventually go beyond just memorizing the rules of storytelling (the cerebral part) to where you acquire a deep down feeling for how stories look, feel, and sound (the visceral part). You'll know when you're finally there because you'll hear stories that don't work and know instinctively why.

It will take time. A lot of time. But if you keep at it, it will eventually happen. It only took me, oh, maybe twenty years? Maybe fifty years? I'm still not that good at it. You're better. It won't take you as long.

Stories are soothing to the soul. It's why little children love them so much. Stories have a beginning, middle, and end. Usually, they start peacefully and they end peacefully. In between, exciting things happen. Your emotional state at the beginning is the same as at the end, only a little better because you have a feeling of satisfaction and are maybe even a little wiser.

More importantly, along the way, even though there is conflict and tension, it's still only minimally stressful because you know it will eventually end. Which is soothing. And because stories are so soothing, I, for one, found myself wanting to hear stories that would soothe me after the deeply disturbing events of September 11, 2001, in the United States.

Like most other folks, my world was completely upended. Which meant I found myself looking around for the most accessible kinds of stories as a means of calming me. Strangely, I found myself turning to football games more than ever before in my life.

Football games are stories. They have a clear beginning, middle, and end. They have a source of conflict that begins with the opening whistle and ideally only ends with the very last play. They have a midpoint where we can take stock of how things are going. They have all the basic characteristics of a good story (or not so good if the game becomes a runaway early on, draining it of tension and conflict).

So what happened with football games around 9/11? They were suspended for the weekend after the attacks. I remember the feeling of deep anxiety in the wake of 9/11. The world seemed to have lost all structure. The American bubble had been penetrated.

Nothing seemed safe anymore. And after a week of trying to process such a completely mentally destabilizing set of events, I found myself craving some form of engagement that would pull me in, yet be guaranteed to have a peaceful resolution to it.

I found this in football games when they finally returned. And as the football games returned, you could almost sense the feeling of relief throughout the nation. They are a form of therapy, operating at as deep of a level as children's bedtime stories. Ahhhh...

This is our starting point for you to begin building a deep intuitive feel for stories. Think of what happens with a football game—how quickly the tension is established, how it keeps your attention, how there is literally a "ticking clock," how the winning team is on a journey that is often led by a single individual—the quarterback.

So many of the basic characteristics of a story. Enough that you can think of a story you want to present and ask yourself, "Does my story have these basic narrative attributes of a football game?" It should.

So let's start thinking about how to begin a story.

TO ERR IS HUMAN, TO BORE IS UNFORGIVEABLE

The late Roger Ebert, eternal movie critic, bless his soul, wrote one of my favorite movie reviews for the painfully bad Leonardo DiCaprio "tedious documentary" (as he called it), *The 11th Hour.* He said, "This movie, for all its noble intentions, is a bore."

I love the simplicity and truth of that statement, which should be taken to heart by all activists yearning to change the world with a "documentary" (or polemic). Noble intentions count for nothing. The goal is to avoid boredom.

So what makes something boring? A simple answer is just the converse of the two axes of storytelling. First, the horizontal axis—if you're doing a poor job with the horizontal axis, you're telling a story that is either confusing, stalls out, or leads nowhere. What could be more boring? Without narrative structure, you're not leading to anything—just going on and on and on.

In my first book, I told the story from my professor days of the night I lectured Spike Lee from the audience for five minutes as one thousand students began chanting, "Get to the point, get to the point." It was the most horrific public moment of my life. My "lecture" felt to the audience as if devoid of narrative structure (I really was working towards a point, I just needed about an hour for it), and thus I was boring. Ugh.

The other, quicker way to be boring is to ignore the vertical axis—to lack humanity in what you have to say. This produces a monotone voice, devoid of emotion or humor. A robotic voice. This can bore people in nanoseconds.

In fact—true story—a friend of mine's wife was obsessed with the famed physicist Stephen Hawking, so when he came to speak in Los Angeles, she insisted they attend. On stage, the host of the presentation asked him questions, then the auditorium sat silently as he typed the answers on his keypad, finally producing a few of his trademark robot voice words every minute. My friend said that twenty minutes into the presentation, he looked over at his wife, who suffers most nights from an inability to get to sleep. She was out cold. Robot voices are boring.

So these are the two main axes for storytelling dynamics. Now let's consider why the telling of stories is so central to broad communication. For this we need to reach into both the worlds of science and art.

THIS IS YOUR BRAIN ON STORIES: NARRATIVE NEUROPHYSIOLOGY

Where does it all start, this storytelling phenomenon? College? High school? Elementary school? I recently accompanied a friend—who works with sharks—on a grade school visit. We ended up in a classroom of five year olds, sitting in a circle, as my friend asked questions. "Do you know how sharks make babies?" and "What do sharks normally feed on?" and "How deep can a shark swim?" All of which were scientifically fascinating questions. But, these were five year olds. Most of them were ending up lost or bored.

I finally said, "Who's ever seen a shark?" Everyone's hand shot up (they've all at least been to an aquarium). Then I asked, "Now tell me the story of the first time you saw a shark."

Everything changed. You could see it in the eyes of the kids. You could even hear coos and purring as they quietly said things like, "Ohhhhh..." Their brains were slipping into story mode. You could feel a calming effect, both from what they were getting ready to tell for stories as well as what they were getting ready to receive in listening to the others tell stories. And you could feel their imaginations fire up. Which was magical.

Stories are magic. And, they are also partly science. So let's take the briefest of brief looks at the science of storytelling.

THE NEUROCINEMATICISTS

Once upon a time, there were some neurophysiologists, including Dr. Uri Hasson at Princeton University. They got so fascinated with how the brain perceives stories that they created an entire new field they call "Neurocinematics." Hasson coined the term in his 2008 scientific paper titled "Neurocinematics: The Neuroscience of Film." It's a fascinating first effort to bring together two disciplines: one from the sciences (cognitive neuroscience) and one from the arts (film studies).

The idea behind it is relatively simple. Using functional Magnetic Resonance Imaging (fMRI), they examined people viewing films. Psychologists and anthropologists have been studying the thought processes of audience members for a century, but not with fMRI capability. Now scientists are able to see the brain activity patterns when people are being told a story versus when people are listening to a bunch of facts. The differences in brain activity are obvious and clear.

At the core of the technique is the index of similarity in brain activity of audience members—a single number that tells if everyone in the audience is showing similar patterns of brain activity or if each other's brain activity is different. It's called the ISC, Inter-Subject Correlation. The clearest demonstration of their ideas can be seen when viewers watch four different types of film: a thriller, an action film, a comedy, and a video of "reality"—meaning just strangers walking around in a park. This is basically a gradient of intensity ranging from the highly intense thriller to the zero intensity reality clip.

The results are clear as you can see in Figure 3. The more riveting the storytelling (with Alfred Hitchcock being the ultimate mass storyteller), the more uniform the brain activity patterns. Which means that when the entire audience is "on the edge of their seats," their brains are firing almost identically. But when their attention is waning, their brain activity is all over the place.

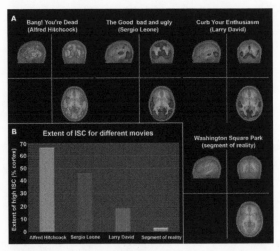

Figure 3. Functional MRI studies by Hasson et al. (2008) showing greater similarity in brain activity between individuals who are watching a Hitchcock movie versus less rigorous versions of storytelling (figure used with permission of the authors).

This is the science that underpins pretty much everything in this book. "Tell a good story and the whole world will listen." When you get to Brian's section, you'll hear him talk about, "When they're laughing, they're listening." I love that basic principle. It's a more specific version of the simple dictum "Arouse and fulfill" that I talked about in my first book, meaning that first you need to arouse the interests of an audience, then fulfill the expectations you have created.

So let's consider this simple question of "What is and is not a story?" This is the beginning of bringing the "critical thinking" perspective to storytelling as we say in the subtitle of this book. It's time to be aware of when you are in the world of stories and when you're not.

TELLING "THE STORY OF THE CDC"

The real start of my developing a "critical thinking" approach to storytelling began in the summer of 2010 when I was invited to visit the Centers for Disease Control and

Prevention in Atlanta (the CDC). Some of the communications folks at CDC had read my book and wanted me to speak with them.

I have a life-long interest in epidemiology. In fact, when I used to teach introductory biology courses I presented, "Disease of the Day," which students enjoyed. For me, the idea of a guided tour of the CDC was like a behind-the-scenes tour of Disneyland (although actually, when you think about it, it's a bit more the kind of place where Pugsly of the Addams family might ask to visit instead of Disneyland—"I wanna see the diseases!").

It's an amazing facility with 10,000 people in nearly 50 buildings. Roughly 500 of the employees are involved in communications. They even have their own television station. In preparation for my visit, not wanting to show up with a blank slate, I asked to have phone chats with a half dozen of the top communications people to get oriented.

One woman in communications talked about the cultural divide between the communicators and the scientists, which turns out to be almost a universal dilemma at scientific institutions. The rift in cultures was brought home by a simple example. She said, "We go to the scientists and ask them what they would like us to communicate to the general public. Almost invariably they reply, 'We want you to tell the story of the CDC.' We say, 'Great, but what is the story of the CDC?' They look at us with frustration bordering on anger and reply, 'You know, it's all the diseases we cure here, the amazing teams of researchers, the drugs we develop...' But, we cut them off and say, 'That's all great, but that's not a story. That's only information. A story begins when something happens.'"

When she told me that, it was, at last, my moment of revelation. It was something I should have learned back in film school. Or at least when I made my documentary *Flock of Dodos*, which aired on Showtime. But it never did occur to me. It took this simple, specific example of storytelling in the real world for me to wake up and absorb this absolutely fundamental starting rule—that you don't have a story until something happens.

Sometimes watching a movie you find yourself, "waiting for something to happen." The fact is, things were happening all along in the movie—the main actor went downtown, scored some drugs, talked to some crooked police, went to his favorite bar. It's not like it's an Andy Warhol movie of a person staring at the wall for five hours. And yet, you turned to your friend seated next to you and said, "When is something going to happen?"

Furthermore, returning to our analogy of the football game, think about how it begins. There is a ritual where the two team captains meet at mid-field with the referees for the coin toss. The audience is willing to give up this small parcel of time. But imagine a game where they tossed the coin 17 times, then the refs said to the spectators, "We need to do this a lot more—we're not really sure how much more—probably until our gut tells us we're set." The fans would riot. "Start the story, already!" they would shout.

THE START A STORY EXERCISE

In our workshop, in wanting to address this basic establishing principle of storytelling, Dorie, Brian, and I discovered a simple yet powerful exercise built around this basic element of storytelling. For one of our workshops, we created the "Start a Story Exercise."

It's very simple. We ask each person to tell the very beginning of a story, either real or made up. They can offer up maybe one or two pieces of "exposition"—facts that set up a story, joined by the word "and"—then they must start the story by having something happen, preferably using the word "but."

The first time we did it, I warned my co-instructors it could be a complete bust—that when we ask the participants to do this off the top of their heads most will lock up and say they need a while to think something up. To our amazement, we

were wrong; all twenty people rose to the occasion, no problem. We went around the room and not a single one hesitated.
Turns out, it's easy to start a story—just ask those five year olds
in the elementary school classroom talking about sharks!

For the exercise, I begin by telling the start of a fictitious
story about myself. "This morning I took a walk in my neighborhood, AND I saw my neighbor watering his lawn, AND
I saw a woman walking two dogs, BUT when I rounded the
corner a man stepped out from behind a car and pointed a gun
at me."

Bingo. We have a story. The first few facts were not a story.
But once something happened (the man pointed a gun) we
have our source of tension or conflict, producing a question
"Did he shoot you?" Now I'm ready to lead you on a journey
in pursuit of the answer to that question.

Once I've established this clear source of tension ("What
happened—don't leave us hanging, did he try to shoot you?"),
I might actually jump to a completely different topic that is the
substance of what I really want to talk about. I say, "I stopped
and froze, and as I was staring at him, wondering what would
happen, I began thinking about the recent ban on handguns
in my city, which made me recall what happened the previous
summer when the bill came up for a vote..."

So begins the true art of storytelling. You've got us in major
suspense—did he shoot you? We'll give you a little time away,
but pretty soon we want an answer to that question. You know
how this stuff goes. Questions need answers: it's the core of
good storytelling.

"The Start a Story Exercise" has proven to be gold in our
workshops, and surprisingly fun—especially when I use it in
large lectures. My favorite moment was a talk to 300 National
Park Service workers in Colorado, where I asked for a few volunteers from the audience to give it a try. One woman stood
up and said, "When I was growing up, I was led to believe that

no one in my family ever did anything famous—no big accomplishment, no place in history—but then one day my mother called me up and said, 'Guess what, we just found out your aunt was on the *Titanic*.'"

Wow! Best volunteer ever. What a great story! Everything she said was pretty boring at the start—the dull fact that she came from an unremarkable family—and then suddenly it wasn't. With the start of her story she had established the question, "Did your aunt survive?" Or, "How did this change your life ?"

Another of my favorites was during my talk to folks at the International Union for the Conservation of Nature in their Fiji office. A man in the audience said, "It was the middle of the night; I was asleep in my farm house and all was quiet, but then I heard a noise. When I stepped into the hallway, I was confronted by a man pointing a rifle at me." The audience erupted (clearly he had started a story) as he shouted, "True story!"

I usually move on at that point, but this one was just too wild, so I said, "Okay, you can't leave us hanging; tell us one more bit." To which he replied, "Only one more bit—the man with the rifle shouted at me, 'Where's my wife?'" Which made the audience laugh and shout even louder.

Love that game. It's like a fishing expedition—you never know what you'll catch, and some may well be whoppers; who knows, it's just an exercise.

Wait! One more. I'll make it quick, I promise. The workshop I did with Chris Keane—he did a similar exercise, asking students to tell the story of, "their darkest childhood memory." I was totally unprepared for this. The first woman who spoke said, "When I was ten, my mother and father and sister and I went on a camping trip. We got to the campsite, unloaded all the gear from the car, then my father got in the car, said he was going to the store, drove off and... we didn't see him for over twenty years." She burst into tears as everyone seated beside her offered up hugs.

Um…yikes. Careful what you ask for when suggesting a theme.

Okay, onward.

HOW QUICKLY DO YOU NEED TO START A STORY?

S o now that we know a story begins when something happens, the next question is how quickly do you need to make something happen? How much time do you get before your audience gets restless? If it's a football game, you get one, and only one, coin toss.

For a story, it's a little more subjective. Let's begin with the assumption that there is a definite point at which the story should begin, the point where the average audience member is ready to whisper, "When is something going to happen?"

Before we try to answer this, let's consider a further question. Do you think the amount of time the audience is willing to wait for something to happen is the same as one hundred years ago? In other words, do you need to start your story quicker today than in the old days?

In 2009, I attended Book Expo in New York City, where they had three editors of bestselling novels on a panel discussion. At the end of the discussion, the moderator asked the editors if they could make one prediction about the future of novel writing. They all thought for a moment, then one of them said that in the future, you won't have forty to fifty pages of set up in a murder mystery before the body is discovered. To the contrary, the dead body will have to appear in the first few pages, as people's attention spans are clearly waning.

Let me take this point a little further with something that struck me in 2011 when I went to see the movie *Contagion* (which was partly shot at the CDC). I was stunned by the opening of the movie. There was no set up. No background about a possible disease outbreak, no introduction of characters, nothing. The movie started with "the story" already in progress as it opened on Gwyneth Paltrow, on a plane, already infected by the deadly virus. No "cut to the chase." We're already in the chase. Which set me thinking.

Granted, this is purely anecdotal. Actually putting together a detailed database to rigorously test this hypothesis would take a huge amount of work, because we would have to control for so many variables, like genre, story complexity, and production value. But still, I think it's reflective of the times.

So I went home and watched two other somewhat similar movies. First, from the mid-90s, *Outbreak*, which is actually a very similar story to *Contagion*, given that it's also about the emergence of a deadly virus.

Then, from way back in the 1970s, one of the quintessential disaster flicks (and prime inspiration for the classic comedy *Airplane!*), the epic disaster movie *Airport*. For each I looked up the total running time then timed how long it took for "something to happen," meaning for the major source of tension or conflict to be established.

You can see the results in Figure 4. Starting with the semi-campy *Airport*, the movie was two and a quarter hours, but nothing significant happened for more than an hour. You spend the whole first hour getting to know the pilots, Burt Lancaster with his career struggles, Dino Martin and his antics while trying to hop into bed with all the stewardesses, as well as the controversy between the airport and neighbors protesting its expansion. Basically, a whole bunch of nothing, until finally, 84 minutes into the movie it's revealed there is a man with a bomb on the flight that Burt and Dino are piloting. Now we have a story; something has finally happened.

In contrast, *Outbreak* in the mid-90s, which is a shorter film, spends 23 minutes setting things up with a little bit of backstory about capturing monkeys in Africa, plus the impending divorce of Dustin Hoffman and Rene Russo—all fairly routine stuff. Then finally, after 23 minutes, "something happens" when Dustin real-izes there's a rip in his biohazard suit, exposing him to a deadly virus.

Then we jump to the recent *Contagion*, the shortest in length of the three, where the story begins on the first frame of the movie. No set up. No exposition. No building of a backstory. Just action—now!

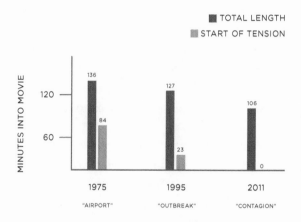

Figure 4. First Act Length Is Changing. This is not a scientific sample, but it is undoubtedly reflective of what we all know is happening as people's attention spans have waned. In 1975, audiences would give you an hour to start your story. Today, Contagion started its story in the first frame of the movie.

We all know what's happened in recent decades. How could it not happen? Narrative dynamics are changing in accordance with communication dynamics. There used to be only three television channels; today the numbers seem almost infinite. People used to wait all day for the mailman to come. Now they get bombarded by email on a second-by-second basis. It's inevitable that people aren't as patient and that you have to start your stories quicker.

So once you decide to start the story, how do you make sure you pull the audience in? It helps a lot if they actually care about what's going on.

CARING ABOUT CARING

Caring is a central element to storytelling. If people don't care, they disconnect. So how do you make them care? Think about the most precious thing in your life—that one person, place, or thing you hold most dear. Once you've got it in your head, I'm going to do something really rotten. Okay, have you thought it up? Can you picture it? Are you feeling its warm glow? Now here we go—I'm going to ask you one, cold, dispassionate, unfeeling question, which is, "Why should we care about it?"

If it is a family heirloom—the broach your grandmother gave to you on her deathbed—my question is the same, why should we care about that piece of jewelry? If it's the wonderful school project your child has spent the entire year assembling, why should we care about it?

I hate that question with the power of a thousand suns. (Which, by the way, is an awesome phrase I'm stealing from one of the "one-star" Amazon reviewers of my first book, who said he hated it that much – it must have hit a raw nerve.) Why do I hate that question? Because it takes me back to the very worst experiences of my former career as a scientist—my darkest hours of dealing with grant rejections.

It turns out that grant writing is, at its best, simple storytelling, and the "Why should we care?" question is central to that entire process. I came to hate the question. I would have to call up people at the granting agency for "feedback" (grrr …) on my rejected proposal, and they would say, "Why should we care about starfish larvae?" I never, ever had a good answer to this question, other than, "Because we need to know about them!" As a scientist, I believed in knowledge for knowledge's sake. I thought that was good enough. And it might have been back in the information under-saturated days of the 1950s. But those days are long gone.

Today, everything needs to pass the caring test. And here was the great cosmic joke that was played on me. After escaping the horrors of grant rejection and vowing to never write another grant proposal ever again for the rest of my life because I was going to Hollywood where such evils don't exist ... I found myself sitting in meetings with producers and movie financiers, talking about my screenplays, and hearing this same question hurled back at me, "Why should we care about the main character in your story?"

I really couldn't believe it. Is it that universal of a question? Yes. It is. So much that you need to consider it in every dimension of every story you try to assemble. And central to this question of caring is the larger question of, "What's at stake?" The stakes are the real drivers of stories.

THE PAIN OF HOME MOVIES

"What's at stake?" is a question asked millions of times a day throughout Hollywood (or at least dozens of times). The stakes are what drive everything in a story. And it's what makes us care.

If your Uncle Roy is bringing a birthday present for you, we'll care a little bit about whether the rush hour traffic causes him to be late to your birthday party. But if he has in his brief case the secret codes for the bomb that a SWAT team is trying to diffuse before it blows up an entire city, we'll care a lot more about how quickly he makes it through traffic. The stakes are higher, so we care more.

In the 1950s, with the advent of Kodak 8 mm film cameras and projectors, the idea of "home movies" first arose. Along with it came instant material for the sitcoms of the day. The term "home movies" became equated with a form of torturing your neighbors by inviting them over for dinner, then pulling out the movie projector to share footage of your kids at the park, your kids learning to ride bicycles, your kids playing in the yard.

It didn't take long for the concept to appear in every show from "Leave it to Beaver" to "Ozzie and Harriet." Everyone knew the problem of people failing to grasp that their interests are not necessarily the same as others.

But the term and concept really is applicable to all forms of broad communication. I've been to parties with hardcore surfers where the dudes will sit in the living room watching videos of one guy after another after another paddling into a wave, doing the drop, carving up and down the face, then eventually falling down. They will watch this stuff for hours while their girlfriends are out on the patio talking. Same deal as home movies. Just because you love watching surfers catch endless numbers of waves doesn't mean anyone else does. Which becomes the perfect segue to this next section.

HBO REAL SPORTS: REAL HUMAN STORIES

If you want to see the issue of "why should we care" addressed skillfully—actually, if you want to see storytelling at it's very best in our world today—tune in to HBO's "Real Sports" with Bryant Gumbel. It's a show that gets beyond the "home movie" syndrome.

If you watch ESPN Sports Center, you'll get the home movie thing, meaning that you'd better be interested in the individual sport they are discussing because, well, the discussion is going to be mostly "inside baseball" so to speak. But "Real Sports" isn't about sports—it's about humans. And that's what most humans end up being most interested in.

"Real Sports" gets to the point where you no longer care what any given segment is about. They only do one episode per month, which is reflective of how they are incredibly selective in their story subjects. And every story has a powerful human angle to it. Usually, if it's about a single athlete, it's going to have a giant arc, meaning it's either the story of some athlete who was at the top of his game (i.e. Boston Red Sox catcher Carlton Fisk or NFL receiver Plaxico Burress) and then made a series of blunders that brought him tumbling down. Or, the reverse—an athlete who seemed to have lost everything but fought his or her way back to the top of the mountain (such as Iron Mike Tyson, who resurrected his formerly incarcerated self into a one-man theater play).

Some stories are just plain miracles that make you cry, like the little girl in Romania who was born with no legs. She was adopted by American parents. But from three years of age she was fixated on gymnastics and on Romanian gymnast Nadia Comaneci, and she became obsessed with her, partly because the girls looked so similar. And then when Nadia won the gold medal at the Olympics and the TV camera flashed to her parents in the stands, the adoptive mother realized the names of the parents were the same as on the adoption documents for the legless daughter—meaning that the two girls were sisters, with the legless daughter having been put up for adoption by their abusive father who was so obsessed with perfection. Nadia eventually divorced her parents, the two sisters connected, and the rest was a blubbering mess for everyone compliments of "Real Sports" and their amazing storytelling skills.

The key point is that the power of their stories rests not in the individual sports but in the human elements. It gets to where you see that the next segment is about the world badminton championships and you say to yourself, "I have no interest in badminton, but it doesn't matter, whatever the story is, I know it's going to be amazing, regardless of the sport."

That is the point at which the storyteller has transcended the constraints of the material. That is the point where the true magic of storytelling comes to life. But again, it doesn't happen if the narrative structure isn't solid. And conversely, if it does happen, if a story does reach inside an audience so powerfully that all their brains are firing in the exact same places as Dr. Uri Hasson (of neurocinematics fame) could tell you they should be firing, then I can assure you that story has excellent narrative structure. It's not a coincidence. It's a causative relationship.

3. CRYSTALIZING THE STORY:
THE WSP MODEL

Now it's time for my most important contribution to this book. I'm going to present three ways to condense your story: into a word, a sentence, and a paragraph. As far as I know, this is an approach that has never been formulated. I have already seen the power of it in our workshops, as I will tell in detail. None of this was in my first book. This is the real deal, folks. It really works. Here we go.

ROUGHING IT IN

My neighbor is a sculptor. When she prepares to carve a sculpture out of granite, the first thing she does is picture the sculpture that is hidden inside the block of stone. She's going to uncover that piece of art that she can already see, but her initial vision of it is simple, not complex. She doesn't see it in all its detail. She sees only the smooth, simple outline.

She then proceeds to "rough it in," carving out the first, simple form. It's the same thing with homebuilders, who first create a "rough in" version of a house, to which the detail is added for the eventual "final inspection."

This is how we are now going to approach the development of a story. In this section I'm going to present three ways to "rough in" your story (though the third one is really in Dorie's section). These are three ways to bring your story down to the absolute simplest of elements, and this is important, because achieving simplicity is both essential for broad communication and the hardest challenge to get right.

There's a famous story attributed to Winston Churchill (as well as Mark Twain, and Presidents Truman, Taft, and Wilson—at least), that when asked to give a speech, he said something to the effect of, "If you want me to speak for only a few minutes, I'll need a couple of weeks, but if you want me to speak for an hour, I'm ready now."

That's the truth. Complexity is easy and quick. Simplicity is the hard part and takes time to get there. It is the main reason we've written this book. Everyone needs help with it. Once you have distilled your story down to these simple core elements, you can then add back the details to get the level of precision you want. But the task begins by achieving simplicity.

A) THE ONE WORD (FOCUS/THEME)

Now that we've established how to start a story, let's take a step back and look at the bigger picture by asking why you're even bothering to tell a story. At the core of this question is, "What is your message?"

That's the more practical question to ask if you're planning to use storytelling to accomplish a goal like win electoral supporters, or motivate people to get behind a social issue, or convince people to support your favorite charity. If you want to connect this question with the more traditional aspects of storytelling, the question is simply, "What is your theme?"

I remember having to write "theme papers" in high school and having no earthly idea what they were talking about. It wasn't until I got involved with environmental politics, learned about the idea of "messaging," and then finally came back around to the literary world and realized, "Oh, yeah, that's the same thing as the theme of your story—what you're trying to say."

In our workshops this ends up being the number one problem we encounter: people excited to tell a story but don't know what it is they're trying to say with their story. One participant told a great story about taking inner city kids out into nature and seeing them come to life, marveling at the most routine of wildlife, like squirrels in the woods, but she had no idea of why this story of discovery was important.

"How would you use this story?" we would ask, and she would think about it, finally saying, "Well, I think it shows how we need to expose kids to nature." Okay, but why? What does it tell us about humanity? How would you use this story to achieve a goal? It's a very cool story and obviously has a lot of potential to be powerful and persuasive, but first, if you want to harness its power, you really need to figure out what you're saying by telling the story. And that is what "theme" is about.

So here's a little technique to help you find your theme.

FINDING THE CORE

This is the story I always tell in the workshop to very specifically illustrate what I mean by the "one word" theme.

In 2006, I premiered my first feature documentary movie *Flock of Dodos: The Evolution-Intelligent Design Circus*, at the Tribeca Film Festival. The day before our first showing, I was on NPR's "Talk of the Nation," discussing the movie, which was exciting.

After I did my segment, I took a taxi downtown in New York City to meet the dozen or so crew and friends accompanying me to the festival. They had listened to the NPR interview. As I entered the bar where we met, I walked down the line of friends, getting high fives, kudos, and slaps on the back for a job awesomely done. Until the last guy—my sales representative for the movie, who was a former high-level Democratic Party election strategist and was very savvy about broad communication. I looked at him, asked what he thought, and he replied gruffly, "You'll get better."

Oof. But he went on to say I wasn't bad, just ineffective and unfocused. I asked what he meant, and he said, "Let me ask you a question, if you had to boil down the entire meaning of your movie into a single word, what would you say the movie is about?"

I immediately replied, "Easy, it's about evolution." Wrong. "Creationism?" Wrong. "Controversy?" Wrong. "Okay," I finally said, "You tell me what it's about."

He said, "'The truth.' That's your one word meaning of the movie. And you need to emblazon that word in the back of your brain. You need to have it ready at a moment's notice for every interview you do from this day onward. If you find yourself lost in the middle of an interview, you can just fall back and say, 'You know, at its core, what this movie is really about is the truth— who is in control of it, how it will be shaped, yadda, yadda, on and on.'"

He was right. He was sooo right. He knew his stuff. And over the next couple years, as I did interviews about the film and found myself running out of words, I was always able to fall back on, "You know, at its core, what this movie is about is the truth—who will shape it, who will control it, how will we defend it." Knowing what it is that you want to say and having it shrunk all the way down to a single word is very powerful in communication.

And as I thought about it later, I recalled the same technique from acting classes years earlier, the idea of finding the emotional core of a scene—betrayal, jealousy, abandonment—and distilling it down to a single word that you plant into your mind to understand at a deep level what everything is revolving around.

If you are lucky enough to be able to do this, it can be enormously empowering. I gave a talk to a group of business leaders in Australia who were involved with their government program that builds centers of business innovation. I tried this exercise, exactly, asking them what is the one word that is at the core of what they are doing. Of the thirty or so people, a number of single words were shouted out, with no significant response, until a man in the back finally said, "prosperity." Instantly, the group came to life with nods and words of agreement. That was the core word. They could take that word and build a communications campaign around it. And then develop a story that brings it to life in a human way. That's how it's done.

This, then, circles back to what I'm saying about theme. It's the same deal. You need to know what your story is about, or, what you want to tell a story about. And then you need to work with material that people actually care about. And if you have a clear fix on what you want to say, then other people can help you by pointing out, "That's a valid message, but the story you're telling isn't conveying that."

A BREAKTHROUGH MOMENT

Let me tell you a little example of how this works. A woman who is a major climate policy expert in California came to talk to me about broad communication. She was very distressed about the on-going devastation occurring from climate change, specifically the increase in intense forest fires in California. I ran through the WSP Model with her. When I finished she had a look of revelation on her face, and I mean like stunned revelation. She said, "I've got it. The one word. It's about 'loss.' I've been speaking about climate change for five years. I've never thought about it in this way. All the stories I'm telling about the devastating changes—they are all about what we are losing. That is my word. Loss."

It was a pretty dramatic moment. That's what focus can do for you. It can be sitting right there in front of you, but until someone pushes you a bit like this, you may have never thought to actually find such a key element that will help you have the maximum impact on your audience.

From the one word, which really doesn't tell the story but helps you focus it, we move to actually telling the core of the story in a single sentence. This has both simplicity and the actual outline of a story.

B) THE ONE SENTENCE (ABT TEMPLATE)

THE GOLDILOCKS PRINCIPLE

We are now entering into the heart and soul of this book, as well as our workshop. As we touch this radiant element, you may begin to feel a tiny bit of circularity, over and over again, like deja vu. It starts with what is sometimes called "The Goldilocks Principle," which is built around the number three. Remember the story of Goldilocks—a story first created by British author Robert Southey in 1837, titled "Goldilocks and the Three Bears" (notice the number of bears)?

Goldilocks enters the house of the bears and begins sampling their stuff. What pattern emerges? It's a pattern of threes. For the chairs, porridge, and finally beds (which, by the way, is three items) she follows the same pattern—this one's too small/hot/soft, this one's too large/cold/hard, and this one (the third one) is juuuuuust right!

This is called "the dialectical three." It's like, "not this one, nor that one, but here's the one that splits the difference." Lock this simple concept deep in your mind—you're going to hear a lot about it. (Brian even uses it to structure his entire part of this book) It's central to storytelling.

It also fits the simple description of our WSP Model. I've found, in trying to explain the WSP quickly to people at a cocktail party, the one word is too simple—there's not much there. The one paragraph (that we'll get to in a while) is very deep and powerful, but takes a while to explain. However, the one sentence ... ahhhhh ... that's the sweet spot. It has the beauty of simplicity, yet also the power of potential complexity. As you'll see.

RAISING HEGEL

Okay, time to get all Hegelian on you. Don't you hate it when you're reading a book and the writer, with a tone of confidence, slips into telling you about some lesser-known figure in the history of philosophy, as if the writer were completely versed in the entire history of western civilization, when in fact, the dude just went to Wikipedia and found a few pieces of trivia.

Well, I'm not that guy. This is just lifted straight out of Wikipedia. But who cares, it's relevant and most of us just don't have the time to get fluent in the classics. That's the whole philosophy of this book: we want to get to the basics as quickly as possible and get to work.

That said, let me give a quick nod to Georg Wilhelm Fredrich Hegel (b. 1770), who, apparently, is often credited with what is called the Hegelian Dialectic. Of course, there is debate whether he deserves the real credit. Regarding the issue of whether or not he came up with it, I say, maybe he did, maybe he didn't, so what. And with that I have just presented what we're going to talk about—thesis, antithesis, synthesis.

The key point is that this is literally as old as the hills. It goes back to Plato and the Socratic dialogues. It's about "the dialectic," as in two sides of an argument, which is pretty much the way our brains are structured to consider things. Basically, gimme the one thing, then I want to know what the opposite thing is, then I'll figure out where I stand. Another way to say this is...

THESIS, ANTITHESIS, SYNTHESIS

This is the language of reasoning. It's the way we best understand the world. Things are clearest when we've got points of reference. They give us perspective. Just like a painting. We can understand a painting in three dimensions if it gives us points of perspective. Three-point perspective in a painting of an alley lets us look at a two-dimensional representation, yet sense the depth in it and understand it in three dimensions. And thus, the antithesis helps us understand the thesis and work our way to the synthesis. All of which underlies the telling of stories.

Which makes me think of Gerald Graff, professor of English at the University of Illinois, Chicago. In 2006, I interviewed him for my movie *Flock of Dodos*, because an article in Harpers suggested his ideas about "Teaching the Conflicts," might have provided the intelligent design movement with their slogan of "Teach the Controversy."

He has made a career of encouraging educators to use controversies and debates as focal points for teaching. In 2009, he teamed up with his colleague Cathy Birkenstein to produce a book very similar to ours, titled, *They Say/I Say: The Moves that Matter in Persuasive Writing.*

In their book they present a whole bunch of "templates" (including an Index of Templates with at least twenty of them, depending on how you count), which are basically fill-in-the-blanks forms to be used in constructing arguments. They're great; it's a great book and with our WSP model, we're basically offering the same thing for storytelling that they offered for argumentation.

Moreover, we're talking about pretty much the same thing—story structure and argument structure. What drives stories is this same basic binary element—two sides opposing each other—two sides in conflict. And that is the key word for stories: conflict.

In fact, Robert McKee, the uber-guru of Hollywood screenwriting, in his masterwork, *Story*, describes what he calls "The Law of Conflict for storytelling," which is that, "Nothing moves forward in a story except through conflict."

How much more fundamental can you get than that? He adds "conflict is to storytelling what sound is to music." Basically, do the math—a story must move forward to work, conflict is what moves it forward; without conflict, a story dies.

So this, then, leads us to what I think could well be the simplest rule of storytelling structure ever devised. Just like Graff and Birkenstein's approach to argumentation, it is a template and it lies at the core of what is probably the most efficient way to tell at least the beginning of a story.

It all begins with a fat, animated kid with a foul mouth, who is basically the Archie Bunker of today's world. You know who I'm talking about, Eric Cartman of the Comedy Central animated series *South Park*. Leave it to him to revolutionize storytelling for today's world.

PRESENTING A NARRATIVE STRUCTURE FOR "THE ELEVATOR PITCH"

Okay, it's actually not Cartman who is responsible for this, but rather his co-creator, Trey Parker. And what this is going to lead to eventually is, to the best of my knowledge, the first time anyone has ever offered up a narrative structural spine for constructing the elusive "elevator pitch."

There are countless books and websites over the past couple of decades that have talked about the elevator pitch. It's the short, punchy version of whatever you have to sell or what you're working on that will come across clearly and convincingly. It's the half minute or so you have during an elevator ride where you are lucky enough to stand next to some wealthy investor who asks you to give him your pitch.

When you look at existing sources for how to create an elevator pitch, one of the unifying characteristics is the need for the pitch to be "concise." Well, yeah. You've only got a short elevator ride. One website says, "An effective elevator pitch contains as few words as possible, but no fewer." Thank you not very much.

So how, specifically, do you shrink down an entire project or an hour long talk into a single sentence that is coherent, concise, powerful, punchy, blah, blah, blah ... all that stuff. The best, most recent source I could find on the timeless elevator pitch is Dan Pink's bestselling 2012 book, *To Sell Is Human*. It's a good and popular book about how we're all salespeople today. The last third of the book is about pitching, improvising (which is Brian's area of expertise), and serving. He opens his chapter on pitching with a cute story about Elisha Otis, in 1853, giving a public demonstration of his invention, the elevator.

Here's how he defines pitching, "the ability to distill one's point to its persuasive essence." I love that phrase, "persuasive essence." That sounds like basic reasoning, which points to the thesis, antithesis, synthesis line of thought. And, interestingly, he looks to Hollywood as "the place to begin." We agree.

He cites the Hollywood tradition of pitching movies as "X meets Y," as in, "it's *Die Hard* meets *Beverly Hills Cop*." And now you realize why we subtitled this book, *Hollywood Storytelling meets Critical Thinking*. He's correct to point to Hollywood for wisdom on this subject, and he eventually even includes among his six forms of pitches "the Pixar pitch," which is a form of Logline Maker (a fill-in-the-blanks template), somewhat like the one Dorie will present.

He also jumps all the way down in size to the one word pitch, and even the question pitch. But what he fails to present, according to what Hegel had figured out long ago, is the structural way our brains are preprogrammed to receive information, which Trey Parker of *South Park* resurrects and even Dr. Neurocinematics (Uri Hasson) supports. There's a three-part flow that is as frictionless to the brain as the proverbial round peg sliding into the round hole.

TREY PARKER CHANNELS HEGEL

In the fall of 2010, Comedy Central aired a short documentary on the making of *South Park*, the popular and brilliantly offensive animated series that by then had been on the air for over fifteen years. The creators have done a phenomenally successful job of telling simple, fun stories that work, week after week, year after year (and, as a total fan, I have spent countless hours watching). When a storyteller spends that much time at the storytelling gym, you expect some mighty powerful storytelling muscles. Such is the case with Trey Parker, the co-creator. When it comes to storytelling, he's a 500-pound gorilla.

The documentary was fairly simple—just an inside look at how with today's new technology, instead of taking three weeks to make an episode as they did in the beginning, they are now able to go from start to finish in just six days. Thus, the title of the show was *Six Days to Air*. But here's where it suddenly got interesting on the storytelling front.

In the middle of the show (which means the middle of the week in which they were following a single episode being created), they walk in on Trey Parker in his office. He's the guy who actually does all the first draft writing—everyone else on the writing staff just tosses out ideas. It's the middle of the night; he looks a little tired as he glances up from his laptop to reveal his secret copyediting technique, which he calls his "Rule of Replacing."

He says, "I sort of always call it the rule of replacing 'ands' with either 'buts' or 'therefores,' and so it's always like 'this happens' and then this happens and then this happens—whenever I can go back in the writing and change that to—this happens, therefore this happens, but this happens—whenever you can replace your 'ands' with 'buts' or 'therefores,' it makes for better writing."

This simple rule jumped out at me. In fact, if you consider our initial premise of this book—that I first came to Hollywood in 1990 with the mind of a tenured science professor, fascinated with how things work and equally fascinated with the power of storytelling—you begin to realize that hearing Trey Parker's rule of replacing may have been the ultimate *connection* moment for me. I marveled at the sheer simplicity of what he said. And when it comes to broad communication, there is nothing more powerful than simplicity.

I've taken twenty years of writing classes, read countless writing books, been in writers groups, read too many books on communication, yet had never heard it put so simply. So elegantly. And here's the amazing part. This simple rule of communication—which granted, I will now modify for more general purposes—comes not from a professor of communications theory or a linguistics expert or a semiotician (whatever that is). No. It comes from a guy who graduated from college, immediately hit it big with an amazing cartoon series (when I was at USC film school in 1995, their original "Jesus versus Santa Claus" Christmas tape was being circulated among my friends on bootleg VHS copies), and has been telling stories for money, day in and day out, ever since. Who is more likely to know the true secrets of storytelling than he?

Why is this? Because he is strong on the crucial side of storytelling—the visceral/experiential/intuitive side. He knows how to tell stories, not by reading books and studying narrative structure, but by simply doing it for over fifteen years, week after week, and receiving the positive reinforcement of money, fame, and acclaim.

Malcolm Gladwell, in his book *Outliers*, chooses the somewhat arbitrary number of 10,000 hours for an expert to fully make the transition from the cerebral memorization of how something works to the intuitive grasp of making the process second nature. Clearly, Trey Parker has done his 10,000 hours worth.

FROM THE RULE OF REPLACING TO THE ABT TEMPLATE

So, after jumping back a dozen times on my DVR and replaying the quote from Parker, and writing it down, and admiring it for the sheer simplicity, I did the obvious thing—I called an actress for her opinion.

And not just any actress, but of course Dorie Barton, who knows narrative structure through and through. She said that, no, she had never heard it put as simply as his Rule of Replacing; however, she is very familiar with what are called "Logline Makers," used throughout Hollywood, and those turn out to be the same thing, just a little more elaborate. (The Logline Maker will be the biggest focus of her section.) But the true ultimate power lies in simplicity, and it was clear the "and, but, therefore" words nail it.

THE NARRATIVE DYNAMICS OF AND, BUT, THEREFORE

Let's now consider these three words in relation to the simplest and most fundamental way to look at the structure of a story—to see it as three acts. You can talk about Acts 1, 2, and 3, but the simpler terms are just beginning, middle, and end.

When you take a closer look at three-act structure, you begin to realize that each act has characteristics: the set up to the journey, the journey, the climax and culmination of the journey.

Stories usually begin with laying out a few pieces of information, called "exposition." As we talked about back in the "start a story" section, a story doesn't begin until something happens. It's okay to begin the process with a little information. The audience will let you present a few facts, as long as you don't go on too long. The simplest and most effective word to use in connecting these initial facts is the word "and."

So if I'm going to tell you a murder mystery, I'm going to begin by saying, "Once upon a time there was a small town in Maine AND a happy family that lived on the south side of that town AND the father was a lawyer AND the mother was an accountant AND they had two children. AND ..." pretty soon it's going to be time to start the story.

GETTING STUCK IN "EXPOSITION MODE"

This is actually a central problem for scientists when they give presentations; they often never make it out of "exposition mode." They never actually start a story, even though they could. I know this all too well from having sat through probably fifteen billion scientific talks during my career as a scientist (at least it seemed like that many at times). Too often scientists will basically say, "Here's our data AND here's a graph AND here's another graph AND here's another graph... AND here's our conclusions."

Which is okay. It's nice and clear. But remember what the neurocinematics folks showed—if you can get your audience into narrative mode, you will get a deeper level of uniformity of thought and *connection* with what you're trying to convey (and there's that title word again, connection). Which means the scientist, and pretty much everyone, after setting up a few facts, ought to begin a story.

So how to get the audience to cross the divide into storyland? The simplest of all words to make it happen is the word "but." It establishes a source of tension or conflict, which is the heart of storytelling.

BUTSVILLE

Just think about the standard thing your friend does to you. She comes up, looks you over, and says, "That's a great shirt, and it goes really well with those pants, and your new hair cut looks great..." Then there's that uncomfortable pause where you're staring at each other, and all the compliments mean absolutely nothing because... you know what's coming next... "Buuuuttttt..."

Furthermore, the word is not said monotonically. It's said with an annoying sing-song, drawing it out, with a tone that starts high, dips low, then comes back up—all of which conveys information in addition to the word itself—adding insult to the impending injury.

When you think about it, you realize that "but" is an incredibly simple word, yet unbelievably powerful. All day long you hear people telling you stories that revolve around this one word. It is the fulcrum to the teeter-totter of life. "My life is pretty good these days...buuuutttt..."

In fact, let's take a moment to flash back to the very start of this book, when I mentioned President Obama's interview with Charlie Rose. Here's what he actually said:

"The mistake of my first couple years was thinking that this job was just about getting the policy right...AND... that's important... BUT... the nature of this office is to tell a story to the American people."

There it is. The "and" and the "but." And now you're wondering, "Did he also say, "therefore"?" Nope. Remember, he's not that great of a storyteller, by his own admission. After this great set up, he starts wandering and ambling.

Once you start to wrap your head around it, if you let yourself, you can get very sensitized to the words, even finding yourself getting self-conscious about using them. You begin to think, "Oh, wow, there's 'but' again," each time you say it. Until you stop thinking and go back to your normal life. Where you naturally say it all day long. In fact, I see that I've used it already 106 times in what I've written so far. It is the bread and butter of our language. Why shouldn't you give it more thought?

So, thinking about the murder mystery I mentioned, we then start the story, having told about the father and mother and children, and then saying, "BUT, then one day the father is found lying dead in the backyard." Now we have a story. Now a question has been posed—Who done it? As a storyteller, I can now lead you on a journey in search of the answer, and the word "therefore" is as good as any to launch us on the journey—"...

the father is found lying dead in the backyard; THEREFORE, a team of detectives begin searching for the killer."

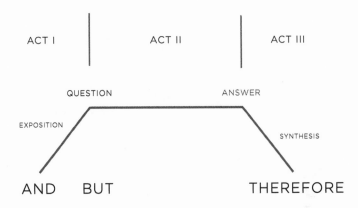

Figure 5. Matching the ABT Words to Narrative Structure. The word "and" is a connector that works well for exposition. "But" begins the actual story, while "therefore" is a good synthesis word to bring things together.

That is the "and, but, therefore", or ABT, that conveys the basic story in a form that is concise, punchy, and lights a fire in your mind. It is also a template you can use to distill down all sorts of large and complex projects and ideas. And if it sounds so familiar that you feel like it's old news that you've known since you were in grade school, all the better. There's a reason Plato converged on the same pattern a few thousand years ago. It's hard wired into our brains.

So is this new? On the one hand, as far as I can tell, nobody has ever put it together like this as a structural device to lead you to the one sentence summary. Buuuuuutttt...on the other hand, as I've said, the concept is part of the fabric of our lives, and there's good reason to believe (based on the neurocinematics work) that the human mind is simply programmed to receive information with this structure. What makes me so certain of this? A year and a half of public experiences with it, as follows.

WATCHING THE ABT IGNITE WILDFIRES

Trey Parker told of his "Rule of Replacing" on Comedy Central in October 2011. By January 2012, I had processed it into the ABT template, which I presented briefly in my keynote address to the 1,000 scientists in a giant ballroom in Anchorage, at the Alaska Marine Science Symposium. I explained the ABT template and then had to leave on a flight that evening. Over the next three days I received five emails from people telling me, "Everybody's experimenting with your and/but/therefore idea in their talks!"

I had explained it to the scientists like this: "Let's say I'm a climate scientist working on ice cores. In Version One of telling you about my research I say, 'I study ice cores in the Arctic, AND here's a photo of my field camp, AND here's a photo of our drilling rig, AND here's a photo of an ice core, AND here's a graph of our data...' On and on with the pieces of information."

In Version Two I say, "I study ice cores in the Arctic, AND here's a photo of my field camp, AND here's a photo of our drilling rig, BUT ... last year a laboratory in Idaho said we're using the wrong kind of drilling rig; THEREFORE, this year we are doing experiments on..."

The first one never starts a story. The second one does and poses the question of "Who is right, the Idaho lab or you?" The presence of a question lights up the mind of the audience member and makes them want to stick around and stay awake, at least until you provide an answer.

The problem a lot of scientists make (and plenty of other folks as well) in not grasping the power of narrative structure is that they will eventually mention the Idaho lab, but they'll put it at the end of the talk—"Oh, and also, there's a lab in Idaho that..." Which makes you appreciate that narrative structure isn't about changing any facts, it's about the sequence of how the facts are presented. One way holds our interest, the other doesn't. Same for lawyers. Same for politicians. Same for the kid at the playground.

A month later I presented the same talk at the University of British Columbia. I heard from a friend a week later that the graduate students were using the ABT template to summarize their research projects in a single sentence.

Then in May I presented it at a conference on business innovation in Adelaide, Australia (the same one that we did the one word exercise with). That evening they held their annual wine-tasting event with 200 conference attendees.

At the start, the man and woman who were the emcees stood up at the front of the room. The woman said, "In previous years we have always held an evening event..." then she passed the microphone to the man who would provide the ABT words starting with "AND..." He handed it back to her. She continued, "the response has always been fine..." He contributed another "AND..." she continued, "that's been okay..."—he delivered the "BUT...", back to her, "this year we thought we'd try something a little more fun..."—to which he finally added, "THEREFORE," and she launched into the details of the wine-tasting event. By then, everyone in my half of the room was laughing and pointing at me. I had no idea they were going to do it. They picked it up from my talk. And why not. It works.

There were several more instances; everywhere it took off like wildfire. Culminating in the TEDMED Conference in Washington, D.C., in May 2013. I was asked to give a ten-minute talk on storytelling. When I explained the ABT template to the organizers, they decided to use it as the focus for their "Great Challenges" discussion groups, where twenty public health issues such as obesity, HIV, Alzheimers, etc., would be discussed. They assigned each group leader to summarize their discussion using the ABT template, resulting in each group presenting a final statement along the lines of, "In our group we discussed this AND this, BUT we realized the important topic for the future is this; THEREFORE, we recommend more work on this."

What was fascinating was to hear the discussion in the group I attended. When it came time to use the ABT template, there was no confusion. It came as naturally as listing the three top bullet points. Everyone seems to feel like they simply know this thing. And yet they don't, really. But they do. And you know what that sort of contradictory feel means—it's intuitive (as opposed to analytical, where it's all been carefully thought through and made internally consistent).

So there it is: an extremely simple, concise, and efficient means of shrinking down any topic, no matter how complex, into a single sentence that is immediately and easily understood. For example, "President Obama had a tight race for reelection AND in general, he ran a positive campaign, BUT in the border state of Indiana they had an opportunity to effectively attack Romney's credibility, THEREFORE they found the story of Mike Earnest, who built the stage from which he was fired." There you go. ABT, accompli.

It might not always work, but why not give it a shot. What have you got to lose?

WITHDRAWAL, DEVASTATION, AND RETURN: THE DEAL CLOSER

Right about the time I was thinking this ABT template was something "old but new," I got the final confirmation from a long-time buddy who was a Harvard undergrad living in Winthrop Residence House when I was the resident biology tutor back in my science grad school days. He grew up to be a lawyer and is one of my best friends. On a visit to his house in

Connecticut, I was seated in his kitchen, telling him about the ABT template.

He suddenly jumped up, spewing part of his cocktail across the counter as his two hunting dogs ran to his side barking, and he shouted, "Hum 9a—withdrawal, devastation, and return—Albert Lord!"

It took a few minutes to get him to calm down, the dogs to stop barking, and me to Google what he had said. Sure enough, Albert Bates Lord was the legendary Harvard professor who taught Humanities 9a, "Oral and Early Literature," for decades. I even found an online article from the *Harvard Crimson* showing it in the top ten most popular courses at Harvard in 1977, a few years before I was there.

When you read more deeply into the scholarly work of Albert Lord, you slowly come to realize it's the same story as *Moneyball*. In fact, a lot of the great debates of today come down to the core of that movie—basically, "Who's right, the number nerds or the gut instincters."

Turns out Professor Lord's great passion was the WDR pattern (withdrawal, devastation, return) in ancient literature. In fact, at one point he claimed to have found the WDR pattern seven times in *The Iliad*. To which his adversaries said, "Oh, nonsense," in the same way that Phillip Seymour Hoffman, the baseball manager in *Moneyball,* says "Oh, nonsense" to Brad Pitt as Billy Beane, the legendary manager who bought into the numbers approach for his Oakland Athletics. Albert Lord was claiming to see a formulaic pattern; the gut instincters were insisting such things don't exist.

The debate is universal—it's the old head versus gut—and in the end it's an interesting debate. Yet it's also as pointless as the idea of Dorie and Brian debating which is more important, the need for narrative structure versus the need to humanize a story. You need both. And guess what the world of professional baseball has come to realize? The sabermetrics school of analyzing baseball through numbers has definitely caught on, but it's not replaced the need for scouts drawing on their gut instincts—only supplemented it.

C) THE ONE PARAGRAPH (LOGLINE MAKER)

The third level of compressing your story is to see if you can expand it to a full paragraph using something straight outta Hollywood, "The Logline Maker." Dorie will get into detail on this.

I'll just offer up two simple things. First, that the tone of it (i.e. "In an ordinary world where...") sounds like a movie trailer, because quite often the logline is exactly what they use in Hollywood to begin making a movie trailer. And second, when you take a close look (it's presented on page 123), notice what's buried in the middle of it—the word "but." This tells you it is simply a more elaborate version of the ABT template.

So I'm not going to go into detail about the Logline Maker, but I do want to give a little testimonial from my generally skeptical scientific mind, which has indeed been won over by its power. This is a "trust me, I'm a scientist," moment. It really is.

The first time Dorie brought "The Logline Maker" into our workshop was with a group of scientists, policy analysts, economists, and lawyers at the Natural Resources Defense Council in their San Francisco office. I had no clue what a Logline Maker even was, except I could see the word "protagonist" in it, which tends to grate against the science, non-storytelling side of my brain. I wasn't going to veto her idea to use it, but I did question it a bit, warned her that most of the people in the group were very analytical, and as such likely to be skeptical of "Hollywood B.S."

She just replied, "lemme give it a shot." As you will see, the Logline Maker is a simple template to help you tell your story in "hero's journey" fashion. So she handed out the template to everyone and told them to give it a try as they filled in the blanks with their stories. What transpired turned out to be dramatic.

About a third of the participants were indeed too analytical to see much relevance. A second third thought it was interesting and a reasonably useful exercise. But the final third, well, let me put it this way, there was an environmental lawyer who plugged her personal story into the Logline Maker then read it to the group aloud. We got to see the transformation before our eyes.

Her logline began roughly, "Coming from a world where few people care about an endangered species of ground squirrel in the Sonoran desert, a humble environmental lawyer is faced with preventing developers from destroying the last crucial habitat for this species, and after …"

I forget how the rest of it went. I only know that this woman was a very professional button-down, high-powered lawyer who routinely takes on the electrical companies and developers out in the desert. She had been largely quiet through the day until this moment, when suddenly, her personal story was coming to life, sounding like an epic Hollywood motion picture on the scale of *Erin Brockovich*.

She and the rest of the group laughed hysterically as she read her draft of the logline, but I'll be damned if it didn't actually sound like a really good movie. And when she finished, the group erupted in spontaneous applause. And when she left at the end the day, she was practically dancing out of the room, saying she couldn't wait to tell her newly formatted story to all her colleagues and friends. And I sat stunned, an instant believer in the Logline Maker.

Futhermore, I spoke to her a year later. The impact was real. She said it changed the way she viewed her entire mission of saving these animals. And along this same line, when I mentioned this anecdote to my good friend Dr. Nancy Knowlton, of the Smithsonian Institution, she said, "Almost every story of

defending nature I've ever heard has at its core the basic dynamics of the hero's journey. There's usually one central individual
who has set out on a mission, encountered the basic elements
Joseph Campbell identified, and eventually prevailed." You can
certainly see the pattern with the classic environmental heroes
like Rachael Carson and Jacques Cousteau.

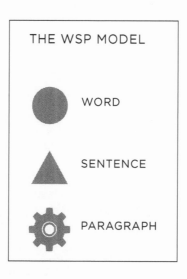

*Figure 6. The Three Elements of the WSP Model. A simple circle for the word, a triangle for
the three ABT parts of the sentence, and a more complex image for the nine logline parts of the
paragraph.*

THE THREE WSP ELEMENTS DIFFER IN SPECIFICITY

Since then, the depth of my belief in the Logline Maker
(and consequently Dorie's knowledge and authority on it)
has further solidified. In a workshop in Alaska, a woman presented her story on preserving an important salmon river. She
used the ABT template, and it came out a bit muddled. She
had multiple threads, and we had limited time for the group to
untangle it for her.

In fact, this is one of the limitations of the ABT template. It's not as broad and general as "the one Word" part of the model, but it is still pretty simple so you can end up with multiple threads stuck in it ("A guy is X and Y and Z, but he suffers from M, which means N along with P, therefore..."). It's not as constrained as the Logline Maker.

Also, the ABT can be used for more than one direction. You could write an ABT for the issue of salmon fishing on a river (meaning the laws), or you could write it about one fisherman on the river. That can be a source of confusion—what exactly do you want to tell a story about?

But an hour later, when she plugged the same story into the Logline Maker—bingo—what emerged was a stunningly clear, simple, and much more *specific* story that again took the group's breath away and brought instant kudos. That is the real power of the Logline Maker, once you know what you want to tell a story about, it can get you down to that level.

The stories are there in so many people's minds, but achieving focus, concision, and structure is much easier said than done. Almost everyone needs help with this process. And this is why we are offering up this small set of tools that we've already seen work so well in our workshops. Now it's time to go further in depth with the process of developing a good story.

4. FINE TUNING A STORY

It's time to talk about molding and shaping your story to maximize its impact. The ABT helped you launch a story. In Dorie's section, she will take you deeper into creating a story that has depth and complexity. I'm leaving that to her expertise. I'll focus instead on some of my simple tips for strengthening your story once you have it up and running.

SHOOT THE (BORING) MESSENGER

I have a lot to say about the horizontal axis (narrative structure), but before we get to that, I want to go back to the vertical axis by addressing the quality of "the voice" that presents the story.

This is the logical starting point, because if the voice is defective, it really doesn't matter how perfect your narrative structure is. And conversely, if the voice is truly charismatic, there's a little less need for the story to be perfectly structured, meaning you would listen to Brad Pitt talk about mowing his lawn, as celebrities often do on talk shows. But don't let yourself fall into the trap of thinking people love the sound of your voice so much they can't be bored—they can.

The most powerful essay of today on the subject of the voice or "the messenger" who delivers the story is Malcolm Gladwell's amazing book *Blink*. He conveys how quickly people pass judgment in today's world and how quickly they shut down if they hear the wrong voice.

For the most part, it's all done and over within a matter of seconds. You hear the voice, you ask yourself if you like and trust the voice, if you don't, then you shut down. More to this point, let me tell you a recent story from the science world that is almost an inadvertent self-played practical joke. It's the story of the organizers of a big conference inviting a keynote speaker who basically negated their entire theme.

A NOBEL LAUREATE POOPS ON THE PARTY

In May 2012, the National Academy of Sciences held a two-day conference in Washington, D.C., with a label that seemed to say everything about their attitude toward communication. The conference was titled, "The Science of Science Communication."

Implicit in the overall tone was an attitude that scientists are conducting so much amazing research on communication, gathering such extensive polling data on the effectiveness of communication, and developing so much theory that they are just about at the point where they can give you a bunch of formulas into which you enter the key variables and bingo, their computers will spit out a "communication strategy" for you that will make you instantly persuasive and compelling.

Actually, right now you're thinking, "Hey, isn't that what the last section of this book was about, presenting formulaic templates to squash your story into a powerful and successful form?" The answer to that question is Brian. That's why he's part of our team. If successful storytelling were as easy as just a few formulas, we wouldn't need his section on keeping things human.

At any rate, that's the idea that organizers of this conference had in mind—that maybe communication could be boiled down to just a few equations. There was even a major talk titled, "Why We Can't Trust Our Intuitions?"

Think of what that means. If we divide overall communication into the two components of cerebral/analytical versus visceral/intuitive, this title seemed to be dismissing the lower half of the puzzle. Which is not what you want to do. And, fortunately, it was eventually pointed out by their featured keynote speaker, Economics Nobel Laureate, Daniel Kahneman.

I'm not sure the hosts had intended for him to, in a single moment, discredit the entire premise of their two-day symposium, but if you ask me, I think he did. In 2011, Kahneman published a rather dense and dry book titled *Thinking Fast and Slow,* which is essentially about this fundamental divide. He breaks the communication dynamic down into what he calls "Systems One and Two," which correspond to the same "gut" versus "head" dynamics that you can hear Stephen Colbert expounding on most any night on his show (he's constantly claiming he's a "gut" kind of guy, driven by his instinct over intellect).

So, as he neared the end of his keynote address, Kahneman said the following words, which provides some of the most important communication guidance possible for today's world. Please read this slowly (when I read books, I usually tend to gloss over chunks of quotes like this – tell you what, if you'll promise to read this slowly, I'll promise not to give you any more block quotes until the very end of the book — deal?) and take his words to heart. And keep in mind that his "System One" pretty much refers to "the gut."

"If we want to communicate with people who are not experts, who are not scientists, if we want to be effective in communication, we should speak to their System One. And that is a different way of speaking. It almost necessarily involves stories. It involves concrete events. You have to assume that System One is largely indifferent to the quality and the amount of evidence. It is bound more by the coherence of the story than by the evidence behind it.

And then I would add something that I think is crucial. Because of emotional coherence, the source is extremely important. The source has to be liked, and the source has to be trusted. And if the scientific establishment is not liked and is not trusted, then the amount of evidence really is going to have very little purchase on what actually happens. Messages from distrusted sources will be ignored, and the amount of evidence will not matter."

- Daniel Kahneman, May 2012

Let's take a moment to let that quote sink in. There's a lot to it.

For starters, consider the source. Literally. You're welcome to dismiss much of what I say because, let's face it, I'm a guy who lost his mind, gave up the security of a tenured professorship and moved to the insane asylum of Hollywood twenty years ago. I'm not sure I trust myself at times. But Daniel Kahneman, he has a Nobel Prize. If not he, then who?

Look at what he says. He endorses our entire message by saying, "It almost necessarily involves stories." Bingo. Amen, Brother Kahneman. (By the way, guess how many talks they had on storytelling at their conference)

Moreover, in the language of our book, his overall message says that what Dorie and I will tell you about the absolute importance of narrative structure is all well and good, BUT, without Brian's section, you could end up simply unheard.

It was such an amazing concluding message to his speech. And consider to whom he delivered it—The National Academy of Sciences—an entire symposium of believers in "the science of science communication." They were there to hear the comforting words that the science is now so powerful we no longer need to worry about dealing with all the irrationality of being human. Wouldn't it be nice if it were that simple. It's not.

CONNECTION POINT 1: TRUST AND LIKE-ABILITY, THE REAL CRITERIA FOR SHOOTING THE MESSENGER

I'm going to hit on a few key, simple elements in this section, which I'm calling "Connection Points." This is the first one.

Kahneman brought it all down to these two qualities of trust and likeability, both of which reside not in the brain but in the gut. They are deeply human qualities. People talk endlessly about their gut feelings of whether they trust and like someone. "I've just got a gut feeling about this guy—I don't trust him." You hear that all the time.

Just look at the Obama commercial with the incredibly aptly named Mike Earnest. They could have gotten whatever Hollywood hunk they wanted to do that commercial. They could have had *People Magazine's* Sexiest Man Alive for 2012, Channing Tatum. He could have said, "Let me tell you about what happened to a guy named Mike Earnest in Indiana..." But would the general public (or more specifically, the voters of the crucial battleground states) have trusted and liked him as much as they did the humble, genuine voice and image of Mr. (whatta name) Earnest?

So this is where effective storytelling in the real world begins. The teller of the story has to be trusted and liked. And that's all I'm going to say on this topic. Except ... (sorry, enviros, for this) ... that if your spokesman for global warming is a former Democratic Party Presidential candidate, it means you already have half of America (the other party) who doesn't trust him. And if Quinnipiac polls in 2004 show his likeability rating as a possible Presidential candidate are twenty points behind the most popular candidates, then you can pretty much conclude that he is neither trusted nor liked by the majority of Americans. So then why would you choose him as the messenger for your environmental issue?

Enough said. Let's get back to storytelling. There are weak stories and there are strong stories. What makes a story weak? Just ask yourself what you say to friends after you've seen a lousy movie. Probably the number one complaint is, "it was boring." How did that happen?

CONNECTION POINT 2: THE POWER OF STORYTELLING RESTS IN THE SPECIFICS

One of the main ways movies (and stories in general) become boring is the absence of specifics. Which means the fundamental rule for you to program into your mind, here at the outset, is that "The power of storytelling rests in the specifics." My acting teacher first drilled that into my head, and then a two-time Pulitzer Prize winner hammered it home with an article I'll discuss shortly.

Let's start by considering the converse of this rule. Why are so many speeches from politicians boring? It's primarily because they tend to be full of generalities (i.e. platitudes), not specifics. So the politician says, "If you elect me, I will do good things." The audience asks, "What good things?" The politician says, "The important good things, the ones we need done." The audience shakes their heads, then somebody asks, "When?" The politician replies, "All the time!" On and on, eluding the specifics that might make for accountability later.

Or the stool pigeon who testifies against his fellow criminals. What do the judge and jury want from the snitch? They want him to "name names." Which is the same thing as "Give us the specifics." With specifics comes power.

Guess what makes you powerful on Facebook? Specifics. I just read a Facebook posting from one of my Facebook "friends" telling in excruciating detail about his prostate cancer. It partly made me ask, "Whatever happened to the old days when people remained hushed about such personal things?" But it also was a demonstration of the power of specifics. The more he told about the specific, painful, awkward details of having biopsies performed, the larger and more impassioned the group of people posting comments became. Had he just made a vague post about, "I've developed some health issues," the response would have been much less. In social media, specifics are the currency.

Specifics are where storytelling gains its real strength. Remember the young woman who told about her aunt being on the RMS *Titanic*. Her first version of it, though already powerful, was still fairly general. Then I began pushing her—"Tell me more about this phone call from your mother telling you this, where and when did it happen?"

"Oh, I was in junior high, at school one day."

And I said, "No, I want to know about the exact minute and exact location."

She replied, "Okay, it was during a break, out in the hallway. A teacher told me to pick up a hall phone."

"And was anyone with you?"

"Yes, my three best friends."

"And what did you do when you heard this piece of news?"

"I started crying."

Bingo. Like an interrogation. You've seen it a thousand times in movies and TV. The witness begins their story with a vague, only somewhat interesting version. The lawyer pushes and pushes, searching for the specifics, forcing them to recall, on and on, until finally, the moment hits where all the specifics come flooding back, and the entire experience becomes overwhelming for everyone. That is the true power of storytelling.

However, what's important to know is that everyone is much more comfortable with generalities than specifics. Generalities are easier to produce and easier for everyone to consume. It's a sort of malaise we all usually prefer, coasting along, nice and easy. Until somebody overturns the whole process.

I saw it with a documentary feature film I did about the Bataan Death March of World War II. I interviewed eight veterans, all in their nineties but still able to recall the sequence of events in early 1942. Having done the "one word" exercise regarding the story I wanted to tell, I knew the key word of the entire Bataan experience was, "abandonment."

It was a tragic situation in which 25,000 American troops were encircled by the Japanese and eventually abandoned by America. In interviewing these last survivors, that was the human story I wanted to hear about—not all the details of casualties and troop strength and movement. I wanted to hear the plain and simple human story of what it feels like to be abandoned, the same basic story that will bring tears to your eyes when you hear an orphan tell about being abandoned by parents. It was the same experience for these grown men, and in fact, they eventually labeled themselves "The Battling Bastards of Bataan."

So I interviewed four of the men, and all I got was generalities. I would ask, "When did you realize you had been abandoned?" in my search for specifics, and all that would come back were comments like, "Oh, I don't know, we just kind of all started feeling like nobody back home cared; you'd hear fellahs talking about it over meals."

Yes, but there had to have been one specific moment—one event—something that really catalyzed the feeling. I finally struck gold with the fifth veteran.

You can hear me on the tape of the interview, pushing this 94-year-old man, not letting him move on, saying to him, "Yes, I know, you felt abandoned, but when—what was the exact day, the exact moment when you realized what would be your fate?" As I'm asking this, he has his head bent over, looking at the floor, thinking, trying to recall. And then he raises his head with a determined look.

"I know. It was Monday, February 23, 1942, huddled around a radio with several men in the jungle of Bataan, listening to President Roosevelt's Fireside Chat, when he finally said there would be no convoy of ships, no armada, no thousands of troops coming to our rescue; the Japanese blockade was too effective, and there never was a plan to rescue the Philippines— that sometimes in war men have to be given up to surrender. That was the day we all realized we had been abandoned."

It was a powerful moment and further strengthened by finding the audio of Roosevelt's actual Fireside Chat and playing it back for the veterans to hear, seventy years later. Very emotional. Such is the power of specifics. And of course this basic dynamic reaches its ultimate height when the number of items is reduced all the way down to...

THE POWER OF ONE (WRITER)

There are countless books and magazine articles written on storytelling, but if you're interested in the practical application of stories in today's world and only have time to read three pages, let me recommend what I think is the most powerful article on the subject. It has the humble title of "Nicholas Kristof's Advice for Saving the World." That's not too ambitious is it?

Seriously, if you consider the ratio of useful knowledge to words, I really don't think anything beats it.

First, it's written by two-time Pulitzer Prize winner Nicholas Kristof, of the *New York Times*. And yet, almost as if to emphasize how much it is intended for the broadest audience, he published it in (of all places) *Outside Magazine* in November 2009.

It's a piercingly clear essay on the faulty programming of the human brain when it comes to stories and how to make those logical shortcomings work to your advantage. I admire the article so much I use it in every workshop and try to read it at least once every few months. It's that good.

The article is packed with wisdom he and his wife have gleaned from years of working in Africa on a public health issue (iodine shortage), and more importantly, from having watched numerous public education campaigns come and go. Out of all that experience, he extracts the patterns he's seen in terms of what works and doesn't work when it comes to educating and motivating the public. Of all the gems of wisdom in the short article, I think the most essential is his examination of the power of specifics when it comes to storytelling.

Drawing on what he presents, let me explain the core dilemma in simple terms. If I told you about a little girl in a village in Africa who is going to die from a disease in the next few months, you would find the story upsetting. If we could measure your level of upset as, let's say 10 units of upset, then if I told you the same story, but this time it was about two little girls who would die from this disease, wouldn't you expect that your level of upset would be twice as much, or 20 upset units?

The sad truth is that it would actually be the opposite – meaning less than 10. And it would be even lower if it's five girls — even less if it's one hundred girls, and eventually hardly at all if it's a million little girls. Kristof cites the famous quote from Mother Teresa that parallels this—"If I look at the mass, I will never act. If I look at the one, I will." And along the same line he points to the old adage: One death is a tragedy, a million deaths is a statistic.

THE POWER OF ONE IN STORYTELLING

The fact is, storytelling is at its most powerful when it is at its simplest—basically the power of one. Which becomes frustrating. Imagine you did meet three little girls in a village in Africa, all suffering from a disease that will take their life next year. When you return home, you want to tell a story that will reach people about the effects of this disease, so you tell about them. But now you have to make a choice: which is more important, combating the disease in general or not hurting the feelings of all three girls?

If you really want to do the absolute most to help combat the disease, you will go with the power of one. This means you will tell the story of just one little girl in such depth and intimacy that we will get to know that girl, feel the pain of her suffering, and end up desperately wanting to contribute to the struggle to fight the disease.

But if you opt to be "inclusive"—to tell about all three girls—yes, they will all feel more included in the process, but your audience won't find it as powerful and compelling. They just won't. It's how it works. You've diluted the story. Sorry. I know it's cruel. Kristof hates that things like this are true, and he says so in his great article, but it's the truth. Our brains have faulty programming.

I saw this dynamic at work at a government science institution that will go unnamed. They hosted me for a day of talks and a showing of one of my movies. But the day ended with what I generally refer to as "a support group for victims of scientist abuse." This happens at many of the large research institutions. You get two completely different cultures at work. You have the scientists, who are very analytical, caught waaay up in their heads, living and working in a largely clinical environment in pursuit of information. Then you have the communications folks, who are from the world of humanities, far less cerebral, living their lives much more down in their lower organs (their hearts with emotion, their guts with humor), yet tasked with the mission of translating the scientists' research to the general public. It can get painfully difficult.

In this group there were about eight communications folks, sitting in a half circle. Each one went through their stories of complaints of how they had been treated poorly by scientists. The last one was a woman who ended up in tears as she told of interviewing a scientist about his research, how he told her about *fifteen* projects he was involved in, she wrote her article, but then a couple days later ended up on the phone with him shouting at her, "I told you about this work and this work and this work—none of it was in the article."

It was true. She had chosen only the three most interesting projects to present. He was furious. And really, she probably should have only chosen one and made it as powerful as possible. But it was beyond him to grasp this tradeoff and "the power of one." It's one of the many communications problems scientists (and lots of other non-communicators) suffer from.

Kristof goes further on this theme to tell about the consequences of adding informational baggage to the process as well. He cites the work of noted social psychologist Paul Slovic, of the University of Oregon, who shows what happens when you tell a good story but then add information to give it a message. If you do three things:

A: tell the story of a little girl suffering from a disease
B: tell the story of a million people suffering the disease
C: tell the story of the little girl suffering, then add on at the end that there's a million other people suffering from the disease as well

We know that B will not be as powerful as A because of what Mother Teresa says. But wouldn't you think C would be more powerful than A—that mentioning at the end, "Oh, yeah, by the way, the story of this little girl is representative of the story of a million people"?

Sadly, no. If you want to keep the impact to its maximum, then leave off the excess baggage. But then you reply, "What? That leaves it with no context, so why even bother telling her story?"

Good point. And such is the plight of humanity. Most people just want to hear the story. They don't want the context. You're imposing on them to put it into the real world. And yet you have to; otherwise, why did you bother telling her story? Just be aware that it all comes at a cost. Context has a price tag attached. Yeah, I know. Strange, and more than a bit depressing. Welcome to the human race.

RAISING THE STAKES WITH "WHO CARES?"

A while back I talked about my most disliked question of "Who cares?" when it comes to the topic of your story. At the core of this question is the awareness that storytelling usually ends up being a competitive process, and the heart of making a story more competitive is to answer this "Who cares?" question powerfully and convincingly. Which I was never good at. But others are, and I've seen them prosper both in science and filmmaking, as it is absolutely central to both.

So what's at stake with your story? Which is another way of asking, who cares? It's a simple process, but it's fundamental to pretty much all stories. You need to figure out "what's at stake" (the survival of millions of people?) and see how you can express it in the most powerful and meaningful way possible. And in the search to energize this question of who cares, one of the most powerful assets is if your story involves any superlatives. What's a superlative? Let me give you the greatest explanation in the history of humanity of what a superlative is.

CONNECTION POINT 3: THE SUPERIORITY OF SUPERLATIVES

This section is the most important bit of writing in the entire cosmos. Or at least that's the idea of a superlative—which is basically a statement of an extreme—as in the most, least, biggest, smallest, loudest, very best.

As a basic rule, superlatives are storytelling gold. They are the difference between "one of" the best things in storytelling and "the" best thing in storytelling. As a storyteller you should have a sensitive ear for them. If you want to tell the story of a bunch of businessmen who bought a huge piece of wetland property for development, the first question you should be asking is, "How huge?" As in, "Is this *the* hugest purchase of wetlands for development in the history of this county? This state? This country? In the world?"

With each level the story becomes more profound, more powerful, and thus of greater impact. With each increment the stakes are basically raised another notch. So we're back to the idea of raising the stakes.

Yet some people are prone to overlook superlatives. Perhaps out of humbleness, they don't want to reach too far. I've seen this plenty in scientists. A few years ago in a video analysis workshop, a couple of scientists from Louisiana showed a great short video of deep-sea creatures they had filmed around the oil rigs. There were about 40 different creatures, each getting a few seconds of video, until in the middle of it all was a shot of an eel-like fish for a few seconds, then a quick flash of *twelve* men on a dock holding up what turns out to be this type of fish, which is *the* longest fish ever collected.

Well, as you can imagine, I told them, "You buried your lede!" (Btw, yes, that's how you spell it "lede"—I know, strange word.) Why not open the entire video with a slow move down the length of that photo of a dozen men on the dock as a narrator asks what sort of exotic beasts inhabit the depths of the oceans, then tell about this, the longest fish alive. It wouldn't be any sort of exaggeration or distortion.

It's the truth—it is *the* biggest fish, and that is the sort of superlative that grabs people's imaginations. Why not grab your audience at the start?

But it's often up to you to get to the bottom of what you have. People mention things casually as being "mighty big" or "god awful long time" or "soo broke." It's up to you to start mining for gold by asking the questions, "How big—biggest ever?" The generality of "really big" is weak. The specific of "biggest ever recorded" (ahem, assuming it's true; please don't force me to give you an introductory lecture on honesty) is powerful. And again, it's all just part of the story development process— seeing what you've got, seeing if you can make it stronger, and seeing if it's in the right place.

And here's a great illustration of the power of superlatives. Graeme Wood, in addressing "The Fears of the Super Rich" in the *Atlantic Magazine,* opens by telling about an ad in *SuperYacht World magazine* for a $125 million boat that is so tall, the ad promises, "Guests will be able to look down on virtually any other yacht." Wood says, "*Virtually* any other yacht! One imagines the prospective owner wincing at this disclaimer," pained at the idea of there being at least one other super yacht that is taller. "Virtually" is not the word you want to see if you're buying an enormous yacht. You want the superlative. You want to own THE tallest yacht in the harbor. Such is the power of the superlative.

SUPERLATIVE VS. PERSONAL NARRATIVES

Now here is where this stuff gets really fascinating. This is about stimulation of your audience, about what stimulates them, and about how that can change over time.

In 2011, Michael Kimmelman wrote an article in the *New York Times* about the changing patterns of visitor interest at the museums of the Nazi concentration camps of Europe. When World War II ended, there was immediately a morbid fascination by the public in the camps where millions of humans were put to death.

Almost as if to hammer home the famous quote about a million deaths being only a statistic, consider what happened in a place where there actually were millions of deaths—Poland in the 1940s. In the article, he quotes Marek Zajac, the secretary of the International Auschwitz Council, who says, "People who visited after the war already knew what war was, firsthand. They had lived through it. So the story of a single death did not necessarily move them, because they had seen so much death, in their families and in the streets, whereas the scale of death at Auschwitz was shocking."

As a result, the initial exhibits featured little specific detail on who the people were and what their individual experiences were like, but instead they emphasized the sheer enormity of what happened. Exhibits featured mountains of suitcases, glasses, prosthetic limbs—everything geared to emphasize the large numbers. People flocked in to gaze in horror at these monuments reflecting the sheer size of the atrocity.

But over the decades the visitors changed. Today almost no visitors know any survivors of the camps or have listened to a first-person account. There is no longer the automatic familiarity with what went on. As a result, the new exhibits have shifted to the specifics and storytelling is used to get visitors to comprehend what happened by featuring the personal stories of individual Holocaust survivors. Piotr Cywinski, the director of the State Museum for Auschwitz-Birkenau, says, "Our role is to show the human acts and decisions that took place in extreme situations here." It is through the decisions that they convey the specifics of the individual experiences.

So when there was familiarity with the story, it was the superlatives that had more impact than the specifics. But once the familiarity was lost, the need returns for the power and specifics of the individual narratives. And the more detailed and specific, the more powerful.

Which leaves you wondering if the same transition will happen with the events of 9/11 in the United States. The major ceremony at the site in 2011 to commemorate the ten-year anniversary of the event centered around reading the names of all 2,977 victims of the event—read aloud by loved ones. It was powerful for everyone. The events, only a decade old, are still painfully fresh in everyone's memories. But will the day come when the number of victims is no longer enough to have an impact, that a new generation will be so far distanced from the events that they will need to hear the individual specific stories in as much detail as possible in order to be truly moved?

NONLITERALISM: TAKING THE PATH LESS TRAVELED

Now let's talk about the various ways to approach a story. As we all know, there's more than one way to skin a cat. (But, yuck, why would you want to skin a cat in the first place? Who made up that saying? I found something dating back to 1840, when maybe cat skinning was common. Heathens!)

Anyway, sorry about the diversion, but it's relevant to the point, which is the role of "literalism," which I talked about in my first book as the need or desire to go right to the point versus being a little less blunt and focused.

It's kind of like the difference between someone (usually a little more European) who wants to find out where you're from by never asking questions, just engaging in conversation that will eventually reveal it, versus me, who tends to not want to waste time, and just blurts out, "So, where ya from?"

A lot of discussion that eventually is productive begins with idle chitchat until somebody finally says, "Let's get down to business." This becomes an important dynamic—whether to cut to the chase or spend a little while off-topic before the chase.

I'm going to talk about "literalism," and not in terms of something like fantasy and symbolism in literature, there are endless books on that topic. No, we're interested in the practical side of how you're going to get people to connect with a subject.

There are two ways. Either you take the literal path and just talk about the subject itself, or you take a less literal pathway and approach it from a less direct angle. The latter is really the true spirit of storytelling.

This is partly what I talked about with HBO *Real Sports*. They don't just sit and talk about baseball. If they're going to have a segment about a baseball player, it's not going to be about how great his batting average is this year. It's going to be about something less literal—about something in his personal life— like he's battling cancer in a big way, yet still managing to excel in his sport. You'll probably learn some things about baseball during the segment, so, ultimately, it is about the sport. But by taking a less literal approach, the segment will appeal to more than just baseball fans.

That's how you reach a bigger audience, by finding something of wider appeal than just the subject itself.

I want to go back to that amazing *Outside Magazine* article by Nicholas Kristof in which he delves into his personal realizations of this same phenomenon. In his case, he was interested in diseases that were devastating populations in Africa that he wanted his *New York Times*' readers to learn about. But he found that when he wrote about people suffering the ravages of a disease like AIDS, his readers, "... didn't really want to read a sad story...because it just reminded them of all the world's miseries."

However, when he wrote, not about the people suffering in a distant place, but about the people over there working to address the suffering, the response was empathetic and overwhelming. For example, when he told the story of a woman who was a rape victim starting a school because she believes education is the solution, he was "inundated with letters and more than $100,000 in checks for her."

This means that the literal approach of just talking about the issue can have limited appeal, but the less literal approach focusing on people taking action and involved in combating the issue ends up being a better story and more compelling. Let me talk about this in broader narrative terms.

MORE LATERAL, LESS LITERAL

In Hollywood, for decades, there was a desire to "tell the story of Mozart." Why not. The guy was one of the greatest musicians ever, but his personal life was not so fascinating. (Actually, can we go with THE greatest musician to make it a superlative? Yes, I know, *LA Weekly* crowned *American Idol* loser William Hung as "The Greatest Musician of All Time" in 2012, but roll with me on this one just to get used to the superlatives idea.)

A good story needs a good journey, and a good journey is the transition from Point A to Point B. Mozart never really did that. He began life as a child prodigy, became a teen prodigy, a twenties prodigy, then exited before age forty, still a genius. Not much of an "arc" to his life.

As a result, nobody seemed able to tell a good story about his life. It finally took the genius of playwright Peter Shaffer (adapting Alexander Pushkin's play from 1830) to tell the story of Mozart from a less literal perspective. Instead of making it ALL about Mozart, he tells the story of his contemporary Salieri, whose life made a very clear and rather sad journey from Point A (the early years where he believed he was as talented as Mozart) to Point B (his bitter later years where he was forced to accept that Mozart was a true genius while he was a mere mortal). That's called "a character arc." It's a brilliant story and illustrates clearly that sometimes you need to back off the topic you're consumed with and see if there might be a more "lateral," less literal, angle to approach it from.

And how do you manage to back off from what you have become fixated upon? How do you manage to find the creativity, the breadth of perspective, the lateral thinking, the moving "outside the box," and every other jargony, buzzworthy catchphrase for inventiveness these days? Once again, Brian.

Honest to goodness, read every word of what he has to say in his section. Trust my instincts. It is the reason I started my partnership with the Groundlings Improv Comedy Theater in 2002, have worked with so many of them in my films and hired many of them to teach improv techniques in my workshops, culminating with having Brian write this part of the book.

Without this less literal element in storytelling, you are doomed to become the bore at the party. It's like they say about the definition of a fanatic—someone who won't change their mind and won't change the subject. Don't be that person. Take Brian's words to heart. He offers up the very essence of what it is to be human. And without humanity, nobody wants to hear from you. Seriously.

NONLITERALISM REACHES ITS ZENITH WITH ZOMBIES AND THE CDC

L et me now tell you of a case study in nonliteralism that will make you laugh with amusement and cry with inspiration. Or at least it does for me.

I love this story. It will give you hope for humanity. It starts with a conundrum—the age-old problem of "how do you get someone to prepare for a threat when the threat isn't present?" This is the question that is constantly asked by the people worried about global warming, and I've heard so many of them answer it by saying, "You can't. Plain and simple. Global warming is fifty years away, there's no way to get people interested in it." Honestly. Which is kind of like that Hippocratic Oath thing I mentioned—no topic should ever be designated as impossible to communicate.

It turns out that at the Centers for Disease Control and Prevention in Atlanta there exists this very problem. One of their assignments from the federal government is to inform the general public on disaster preparation—how to get prepared for everything from hurricanes to floods to fires to earthquakes. Their general motto is "Make a plan"—meaning have your house stocked with the basic disaster needs and make sure everyone in the family knows what to do in the event of a disaster. But how do you get a family motivated to do this when the threat isn't imminent?

At CDC every year, the task fell to a few unlucky communications folks to do "this year's disaster preparation effort," usually in May in advance of hurricane season. It had just become institutionally accepted that you made a website, sent out some brochures, it all fell on deaf ears, and then the day before a hurricane shows up everyone makes their mad dash to the stores to buy emergency supplies—exactly what you're trying to avoid. But then there came a spark of innovation.

Three brave souls in Communications, headed up by the very energetic and creative Dave Daigle, came up with a simple revelation. They realized that all the supplies and planning you need to be prepared for a hurricane, flood, fire, or earthquake were just the same things you would need to be prepared for— (drum roll, please)—an attack of zombies. When the day comes.

Being a large government organization with many layers of bureaucracy, they knew that as brilliant as this idea might be, the odds were it would have to go through many committees for approval until it was finally transmogrified into something inert, innocuous, and ineffective. Large organizations have a way of doing that.

So they spent a couple weeks pondering how to keep their delicate and ingenious idea intact, yet also get it implemented in the real world. They finally hit another realization: that there are a few senior scientists at CDC who have their own blogs and are not required to submit their content for review before posting.

They went to one of them, Dr. Ali Khan, and convinced him to make just the tiniest of blog posts on a Monday morning about how preparing for a zombie apocalypse was just like preparing for any other disaster. He agreed; he posted the simple tongue-in-cheek blog that morning, and over the next couple days they received a few comments and emails chuckling about it, but nothing big.

TURNING $87 INTO $3 MILLION

Until Tuesday evening. That's when the wife of a major risk management expert in New Jersey, who often works with CDC, spotted the blog post and was impressed by it. She innocently sent an email to Tom Frieden, the director of the entire CDC, complimenting him on the creative communications work taking place there. He had no idea what she was referring to, but he noticed she mentioned Ali Khan, so he forwarded the email to him.

Dr. Khan forwarded that email to Dave Daigle and his group, they took that as the "green light" for their project, and on Wednesday morning began tweeting and posting on Facebook about Zombie preparedness. By midday, the CDC server was inundated with views—thirty thousand on a single page. By that afternoon the Atlanta Fox News Channel called up saying, "There must be either a hoax or a hack going on because people at the CDC are talking about zombies."

That night the *Wall Street Journal* ran an article. The next day a person in a different part of Communications at CDC called a reporter at the *New York Times* to discuss a story they were pitching to them about the ten biggest public health crises of the last century, but when the reporter got on the line he said, "I want to talk about this zombie story," and that's exactly what he wrote up

Figure 7. The Zombie Disaster Preparedness Kit from the Centers for Disease Control and Prevention in Atlanta. A little bit of creative thinking produced a lot of disaster preparation.

Within a couple of days, friends were sending me articles about the CDC Zombie Disaster Preparedness Kits, asking me—knowing that I had been running workshops at CDC—if it was my idea. "Seems like the sort of craziness you'd think up." But I would write back, "Are you kidding—I'm nowhere near that creative—they are communications geniuses."

The media activity turned into a veritable mushroom cloud over the next month. By mid-summer, the CDC's media analysis company, Cision, estimated that the singular idea of zombie preparedness at the CDC had generated at least $3 million in free media exposure.

As Dave Daigle says, just on ABC-TV alone, a thirty-second commercial costs $94,000 to air in prime time. Yet ABC News did two stories on the blog of several minutes each, which didn't cost CDC a cent.

And, in fact, to put icing on the cake, Daigle estimated their entire zombie effort cost a total of $87, for stock photography used in the blog. By September, they had been nominated for five Platinum PR Awards—the big annual showcase for public relations firms across the country. They attended the ceremony in New York and, up against the likes of Ogilvy and other big hitters, they won two of the awards, including the "Wow Innovation Award." All of which warms my heart to the greatest extent possible. Such is the power of creativity, innovation, and good ideas. This is the very reason improv is so valued in the higher levels of the corporate world, as Brian will tell about. It is the process that opens your eyes to the good ideas sitting right before you. Like zombies.

AND WHAT ABOUT AFTER THE ZOMBIE DUST SETTLED?

O kay, what are you, some kind of scientist? Let me guess. After all that excitement, you want to be the party pooper by asking, "Yeah, but did the CDC zombie movement ever translate into action? And if so, I wanna see the metrics—show me the numbers." (Piece of advice if you want to be seen as a tough guy in the media world, just ask for "the metrics," even if you don't know whether they matter.)

Actually, you want to see what an obsession with "the metrics" gets you? Just look at the failed American climate movement that squandered over $1 billion dollars trying to create enough momentum to pass legislation. Numerous reports in the past couple of years reported the post-mortem of the movement and blamed much of the failure on the overly cerebral, overly cautious approach of the foundations who generally refuse to support anything unless backed up by "metrics."

In the case of zombie preparedness, just look at it from the reverse perspective—I ask you to prove that you can score $3 million in media exposure and not have lots of worthwhile things happen. The overall list of what they accomplished is hard to quantify, but it starts by "pegging" the entire subject of disaster preparation to a national holiday—Halloween. Just watch the media in Atlanta now around Halloween. You'll see lots of zombie stories, and many will include the CDC.

Moreover, the CDC was founded in 1946. The first zombie movie is believed to be Victor Halperin's *White Zombie* in 1932. That's a lot of years of both zombies and CDC living in the same country but with no clear connection, until Dave Daigle came along. Now the two go hand in hand—ever since the disaster kits. Every year since 2011, Dave and others from CDC do a panel discussion at the gargantuan Dragon Con in Atlanta, which draws a large audience.

As for metrics ... two research institutes have offered to do the study that's needed to determine the exact impact of the zombie kits. But they've asked for a budget of $250,000. As Dave says, "I'd rather spend that money to make more materials. We know it's popular. We know kids love the campaign. And they are the drivers of their parents."

Sometimes you still gotta go with your gut instincts.

5. END OF STORY

IT'S BEEN A "ROUGH" RIDE

So you're thinking, "We're already at the end?" Seems like we're only a little more than a third of the way through the book. How can we be talking about ending the story?

Actually, you're only at the end of my coaching session on how to "rough in" your story. I've given you some tools to take your idea and shrink it down to the simplest, most concise core elements.

I've got two more things to cover, and then I'm going to hand you over to the specialists who will take you to a deeper understanding of the elements I've sketched out. And keep in mind what I told you about "the power of storytelling rests in the specifics." The specialists are the ones with the specifics, which means you're headed to the powerful stuff.

But first, a final bit about how your brain works.

NOW THAT'S ENTRAINMENT!

Let me tell you about a rather bizarre experiment we inadvertently did in our first workshop.

First, how long do you need to tell a story? Could you tell a story in one minute? Could you do it in half a minute? What about ten seconds? How about a mere *five* seconds? Could you tell an entire story with a beginning, middle, and end in just five seconds?

A few years ago, a website called Five Second Films appeared. At first my friends and I thought it was a joke. And actually, in truth it is kind of a joke because just about all the videos are hilarious. But the website is real, and most of the videos really do manage to tell a complete story in just five seconds.

For example, their most popular five-second video ever is titled "Late for Work." It's a very simple piece. We see a guy asleep in bed, we see his alarm clock click on, we see him look at the time with fear, we see him sit up and shout, "Oh, *fuuuuuuuu*—" then we get a rapid cut montage of him driving to work, at work in an office setting, and all day long continuing his shout of, "—*uuuuuuuuuu*—" then finally we see him at home at the end of the day, getting undressed for bed, and in the final shot falling back down in his bed, finishing the word, "—*uuuck!*"

The film is brilliant, hilarious, and flies by in the blink of an eye. It's only five seconds. Yet it has a very clear beginning, middle, and end. Thus proving how cleanly you can still tell a story in just five seconds. It's amazing. I love it. And I love Five Second Films.

So in our very first workshop I decided to show a collection of twenty Five-Second Films, which takes only a little over two minutes to watch. They are all funny, and most of them are outlandishly crude. Like, "yikes" level of crude. The group of twenty participants exploded and screamed with laughter at about half of them. It was a real shotgun experience, with two or three missing the mark, then one hitting everyone from a different angle and everybody bursting out howling with laughter again. Really wonderful.

But here's the crazy part. When the madness ended, everyone was talking differently. Welcome to the weird world of "entrainment."

At least that's what I'm calling it. I recall the word from the study of fluid mechanics, where it describes the process of a particle getting pulled into a moving current. It is said to be "entrained" in the current, or moved along. And that's what we're talking about. You get entrained by the environment in which you exist. Let me put it this way.

If I were to put a microphone on you and take you to a retirement home, then listen to the recording of you talking, we would hear you speaking quietly, slowly, clearly—"Hel-lo Missus Jones ... how ... are you ... today?"

But if I took you to a crowded, kinetic Hollywood cocktail party, we'd hear you talking rapid fire, "Dude, whatsgoingon? Where've you—oh, look who's here ..."

That's entrainment. You've been pulled into speaking at a certain speed by the environment you've entered. And that's what we saw with our group after subjecting them to twenty Five-Second Films. When they went back to talking about their films, you could hear their thinking was substantially different. They seemed wound up. Not just talking faster, but also thinking in faster terms with regard to their stories. Instead of having a bunch of exposition, they were starting their stories right off the bat.

This happens. People's thinking acclimates to the local environment. You see this with film editors. Feature editors and trailer editors tend to be two completely different species. If you have a feature editor (someone who edits two-hour long movies all day) put together a trailer for a movie, it will probably be clear and tell a good story, but it will be a little on the slow side. Conversely, if you were to try hiring a trailer editor (who spends all day putting together super high energy, rapid-cut, whirlwind, two-minute trailers) to edit a feature, the person would probably just lock up after a while and say, "I'm sorry, but I just can't hold my focus for that long."

So the relevance of all this is that you can entrain your brain to a certain pacing. Force-feed yourself a bunch of short, high-energy films and you will think in that mode. Watch a bunch of long, slow-moving movies and you'll get into that mode. It's like playing tennis; you tend to mirror your opponent. If your opponent plays well, you will look good even if you lose. If your opponent is lousy, you'll look lousy even if you win. You'll get entrained.

A last comment on this is that recent neurophysiology research is shedding light on so-called "mirror neurons," which could be a part of this phenomenon. The suggestion is that there exist neurons in parts of the brain that enable one person to "mirror" the activity of another. But I have to say I'm hearing a lot of cautionary warnings from the better science journalists I know about the increasing gulf between neurophysiology scientific research and the popularization of it by writers.

It's basic storytelling dynamics. Popular writers like to tell big stories. Scientists like to tell the truth. When I spoke with Dr. Neurocinematics, Uri Hasson, he emphasized repeatedly how limited their findings are. I've heard others comment on how crude functional MRI is as a tool for brain activity.

Yet, you find lots of popular science writers rounding everything off and telling simple "gee whiz" stories of how the neurophysiologists are figuring out how everything works (rising New Yorker writer Jonah Lehrer lost his career by falling victim to this). They aren't. Yet. So the vibe I sense for mirror neurons is "too soon to tell."

STORYTELLING IS AN EVOLUTIONARY PROCESS

This is my second final point, and I don't mean it descriptively (as in, "storytelling is something that has evolved from the cavemen," though it probably has). I mean it functionally, in terms of how you make your stories effective. You need to evolve them over time.

Which calls for another story from the Bataan movie. I interviewed eight of the last survivors who were there, including Dan Crowley, a 90-year-old wild man from Hartford, Connecticut, with the energy of a twenty-five-year-old—I swear. It wasn't even much of an interview. We showed up, he dragged us out to his backyard, we set up the camera, and he was off like a rocket. Not an interview, more of a monologue for a solid hour as he told one story after another.

What was amazing about his stories is they had almost perfect narrative structure. Each one—"We were doing this, *and* this, *but* then this happened; *therefore*, we ended up doing this."

Not that he used those words exactly, but the structure was just about as good. On and on. In the same way that Albert Lord said he saw seven instances of "Withdrawal, Devastation, Return" in *The Iliad*, I'm sure there were at least seven instances of "And, But, Therefore" in Dan's hour of wild stories that included refusing to surrender to the Japanese on Bataan then swimming to Corregidor Island to fight another month only to have to surrender there. Absolutely riveting stories.

Then at the end of the hour he made his way through the Japanese surrender at the end of the war, his return home, and his story finally ended. So at last, I started my "interview" by asking him a first question. Guess what I got back. More or less nonsense. No stories. No narrative. Just a bunch of rambling. For every question, until I finally drew it to a close after twenty minutes.

On my drive home I began to realize what I had just experienced. His amazing stories have perfect narrative form because he has been telling them for decades—since 1942, when it all happened to him. He loves telling the stories, so you know he's told them all, over and over and over again—at cocktail parties, at family gatherings, and at neighborhood picnics. And with each telling, he's engaged in the interactive aspect of storytelling by watching and sensing his audience. Taking in feedback. Realizing that when he told about the trucks that slowly drove down the hill, everyone would start to glaze over. But when he told about the cannon fire that began to blow up the trucks, he could feel everyone draw in. So over time, he trimmed the driving, expanded the explosions.

STORYTELLING: IT'S AN INTERACTIVE PROCESS

So that is the interactive nature of storytelling. You can't sit alone in a room for years, making up your stories, then expect to unleash them on the public and have major success. It might happen, but the odds are mighty slim.

Comedian Jerry Seinfeld took part in a great documentary in 2002, aptly titled *Comedian*, in which they followed him to small comedy clubs working on new material for his stand-up comedy act. He talks in detail about the difficulty of developing good material. Storytelling and joke telling are pretty much one in the same. You have to develop the material, then you have to "evolve" it over time.

Which means this is my final piece of advice to you—work through the WSP process, then take your material out to gatherings and get to work, like this...

You: I'm working on this election campaign. We're developing a story about our opponent.

Friend: Really, what's the story about?

You: Deception. (THE ONE WORD)

Friend: Whoa. Like how?

You: Like giving hard-working folks the impression you're there to help them, only to destroy their lives.

Friend: Yikes. This sounds bad. So what's the story?

You: It's about this factory where they asked some guys to build a stage, *and* the guys built it, *but* then three people from a takeover company showed up and told all the employees they were now fired; *therefore*, their lives were destroyed. (THE ONE SENTENCE)

Friend: Day-yamn. That's harsh. Tell me more, where did this happen, what was the company...

You: Well, for starters, the nation was in a recession already *(Ordinary World)*, and a trusting factory worker named Mike Earnest *(Flawed Protagonist)* was one of several guys told to build this stage *(Catalytic Event)*, and when..." (THE ONE PARAGRAPH)

That needs to be you. You can do it. You ask yourself what is the one thing you want to convey to an audience. Put that into a word. Go out and find the story that matches that word. Put your story into the ABT template. Then look at all the variables for the Logline Maker that Dorie is going to tell you about. Go back and determine each one of those as best as possible. Then get yourself out to the social circumstances where you can start telling the story. Not reading it off a sheet of paper, but actually telling it like a performance for which you're studying the faces of the group, gauging how interested they are, taking in their feedback, revising it, then trotting it out at the next social event.

Slowly, over time, you will get there. You'll have a good story.

We absolutely do live and breathe stories, day in and day out, in all walks of life. We can't all be perfect storytellers, but we can all get better, and it starts by having a working knowledge of how stories work. And on that note, I shall now hand the floor over to my two very talented colleagues. Take it away, Dorie and Brian.

DORIE BARTON

DORIE BARTON has been a professional actor in the film and television industry for twenty years, and a script consultant and writing coach for fifteen. Her work as a consultant and coach has led her to story development work with screenwriters, filmmakers, novelists, literary managers, and production companies, working on independent and studio projects, and both narrative and documentary films. Her work on camera as an actor has included several television series as a regular and recurring character, numerous guest star roles, and work in independent and studio pictures. She is also a multi award-winning stage performer, and has been a member of the esteemed Evidence Room theatre company since 2001. She holds a BFA from the renowned California Institute of the Arts, created by Walt Disney to provide artists with a well-rounded education in all art forms.

2. NARRATIVE: HEROES OF HOLLYWOOD

PART ONE: WELCOME TO STORY

The fact that Randy calls me the "cerebral" part of the team makes me laugh since I've spent much of my life being looked at as a "flaky actress." That's okay. I'll take it. I often tell folks that I know an enormous amount of information about a very tiny subject, which I guess is probably what most of you are like. Specialization is a beautiful thing.

For the next little while, I'm going to walk you through my part of the world: Story, with a capital "S." I'll give you a blueprint, a tool kit, and some directions for making a story of your own that hopefully won't make you want to pull your hair out like when I tried to assemble a giant iron daybed from Ikea by myself. I'm here to help.

We're going to talk about the components of Story, what they mean, and how to use them. And whatever kind of story you want to tell...be it fact or fiction, whether you know right now what you want it to be, or if you'd rather do just about anything than face the dreaded "blank page"...I'm going to make it nice and easy for you. Hopefully, you'll have some fun along the way. Helping people find their stories is my favorite thing in the world.

Most importantly, what we're hoping to do here is to show you that the building blocks of film stories, which have been used with repeated and indisputable success for over a century, are the same building blocks that will help you tell your story, whatever field you're in. Maybe you want to get people excited about a citywide Ride-Your-Bike-to-Work day. Maybe you want to convince a dangerously overweight patient to eat healthier food and exercise to save their life. Maybe you want to instill in your community the passion for urban agriculture.

The skills that screenwriters and documentary filmmakers use to develop stories for the cinema are the same skills you'll use in crafting your own story. Whether you want to inspire, educate, advocate, or even just break the ice, by the time you're done with this book, with everything that Randy, Brian, and cerebral-me will share with you, you'll never be in the dark again when you hear the word "Story." You can do it.

SO, I'M EIGHT...

I have a very vivid memory: I was eight years old. I wore thick glasses and hand-me-down clothes. I loved books and would read everything I could get my hands on. Now my family, an Army family from the Midwest, went to Methodist church, so I grew up thinking church was pretty much about standing up and singing. Loud. But it was also about stories. Church was filled with all kinds of stories. Scary ones. Joyful ones. Bloody ones. Spooky ones.

So I'm eight. I'm curled up in the scratchy green armchair in the living room, I'm reading this big, fat copy of Edith Hamilton's *Mythology*, and a sudden dawning came into my mind. I yelled to my mother in the kitchen, "So these stories in this book are just stories the Greeks and Romans made up to explain things they didn't understand, right?" My mother patiently said, "Yes." "But the stories at church, they really happened just like they say?" And my education-loving but rule-abiding mother answered, "...Yes." To which I said, "'Cause they sound a lot alike." My poor mother.

I feel lucky to have found out that truth so early in life: All stories—real or imagined, fantasy or fact—are basically the same.

That's not limiting. That's liberating. That's terrific news because it means we all know how to entertain, teach, explain ideas, and learn from each other's mistakes all using the same basic tool: Story.

I grew up on a steady diet of gritty action movies with my dad, and with my girlfriends, every musical put on film. I loved *Dirty Harry* and *The Harvey Girls* equally. I started seriously studying theatre just before high school and fell in love with the stage. Throughout high school, and during my time at the California Institute of the Arts, I had a growing awakening about the nature of Story.

As an actor, and in my story consulting work over the past many years with producers, filmmakers, writers, and—lately—scientists, I've come to understand the meaning of Story more clearly.

Story is a set of details about a person's (or persons') experience, arranged in a deliberate structure, which gives it specific meaning and universal appeal. Story structure is a process in which a hero does something challenging in order to gain something crucial.

That's it! Simple, right? Okay, not right off the bat. But with a growing understanding of what makes a story and how to give it structure, everyone can learn good storytelling.

In my mind, Story is very much like architecture. A house must have walls that support a roof. There should be a doorway. Perhaps a door. But other than those basic things, a house can be anything from a yurt to Versailles. It's all in the details.

The great thing about Story is that no matter what you're starting with, no matter how disparate the ideas seem, or how clinical, seemingly boring, or dry...there is always a story in there once you learn what a story is made of.

Our time here is meant to help you understand what Story is, so you can use your own details and build the story that says what you want it to say, in the way that people will best be able to hear it.

And ultimately, it is that simple. I've seen lots of people make that happen.

A STORY FROM SEEMINGLY NOTHING

One of my favorite experiences as a writing coach was when a talented writer came to me for help with a new piece of fictional material based on her family. She had just been home for the first time in a long time and had had an eye-opening experience. We talked through a whole host of ideas that were fueling her creative impulse: the history of her family, how slippery memory is, how buried the truth can get. She said she felt like she just had this big pile of emotional "stuff" and had no idea what to do with it or where to start. All she really had was a feeling. A feeling that she had just really seen her family for the first time.

Through the process of working closely together, we applied the basic principles of story structure, slowly building in ideas that expressed that feeling. Before long, she had written a sharp, emotionally raw piece of material that bore no resemblance to that pile of "stuff", but was completely authentic to what inspired her in the first place. The story also happens to contain some valuable information about the issues of compulsive hoarding, Sundowner's Syndrome, hydraulic fracturing... but because the emotional impact of the story is so strong, you don't even notice that you're also learning something. The finished script is an incredible piece of personal-cum-public art that will be made into a movie next year.

While some of you might have a great deal more information to cull through to make a story, others might have as little as an intention, a desire to share something, a single experience. Even if all you have is a feeling about something, you can make it into a powerful, effective story. It takes hard work, maybe some blood, sweat, and tears, but it's there, waiting for you to mold it.

WHAT WE DO

Nobody knows Story like Hollywood. Telling stories is literally all we do. And we don't just tell stories. The culture of Hollywood itself has a narrative. We have the myth of the "falling star struggling for relevancy." The myth of the "bad boy actor redeemed by hard work, good luck, and the love of a good woman."

Story is *the* Hollywood product.

But the concept of story is everywhere now. The word "narrative" has become part of our broader culture and is showing up ubiquitously. The science of narratology is being applied to multiple fields of knowledge. Everyone wants to know what the narrative of something is. The narrative of a company. The narrative of a war. The narrative of an economic phase. The narrative of a populist uprising. The narrative of a scientific discovery.

Higgs boson, the Arab Spring, and the NRA all have narratives. It's just out there.

A LEAKY FAUCET

It's hard to be a person living in the 21st century and not know that Story is how we digest and interpret events, big and small. There is a great deal of advice out there about how to connect with audiences and be persuasive. It all points to telling a story, conveying the right narrative.

But there's almost no solid information about how to do that. It's all well and good to convince people they need to tell a story, but if you don't tell them how, they can't do the job. It's like saying to stop a leaky faucet you just have to fix it. How? What do I need? A screwdriver or a wrench?

But here, in the land of the storytelling business, we know how to make a story that works. We're very good at it. Hollywood is not the carnal, depraved, mental wasteland that it tells you it is. That's just another good story. We're people with car payments, families, and dogs, just like you. For the most part, we're craftspeople, and we only make one thing.

In Hollywood, there's a very basic system for creating a story. It's the same system for every story. In fact, it's always the same story.

A (VERY) BRIEF HISTORY OF STORY

The first person we know of to formally recognize the patterns in narrative is Aristotle, and his slim treatise *Poetics* is what we all owe a huge debt to in understanding how humans like to tell and hear stories. He broke down what was similar in each of the tragic plays he loved, and why those elements were so effective. Greek drama had a definite structure to it, and the devices used over and over again had a profound effect on the audience: catharsis. Aristotle recognized that just by watching something tragic, audiences grieved, learned, and worked through powerful emotions. The stories were so well crafted that they connected on a primal, visceral level, and they allowed people to experience strong emotions without having to actually go through what the characters experienced.

People don't need a story to be true for it to be powerful. In fact, there's plenty of evidence just from watching a group of people get worked up when the subject of *Downton Abbey* comes up. Gossip flies. Opinions get heated. You'd think these were their family members they were talking about. Great storytelling, fact or fiction, cuts right to the heart. It gets people excited.

THE MONOMYTH

In 1949, a little over two thousand years after Aristotle, Joseph Campbell made his life's work in comparative mythology and religion accessible to the broader audience by writing the seminal work *Hero of a Thousand Faces*. Campbell's work is powerful for many reasons, but at the core of his contribution is what's called the Monomyth.

What Campbell had discovered by studying the myths, fairytales, oral histories, religions, and fables of cultures all over the world was that—amazingly—we're all basically telling each other the same story over and over again. No matter where people live, no matter what they're trying to explain, no matter what the details are...there's an innate pattern that emerges.

The Monomyth has become almost a self-fulfilling prophecy. We see the pattern, and we see our powerful emotional response to stories that follow this pattern. People, for myriad reasons, like to hear stories that are told this way.

Because it's well known now that people like to hear stories this way, and have strong emotions arise from hearing stories this way, we now know that we should *tell* stories this way if we want to get the desired response. And because we're telling stories in the pattern that people respond to, people keep responding, so we keep telling.

THE HERO'S JOURNEY

Over the course of time, the pattern has become very refined. Here in Hollywood, and elsewhere in the humanities, we usually call it **The Hero's Journey**, after Joseph Campbell. In 1988, a documentary series and accompanying book by Bill Moyers, entitled *The Power of Myth*, about Campbell's work, and a 1992 book by Christopher Vogler, *The Writer's Journey*, made the Monomyth's concepts more accessible to the broad public and the screenwriting community, respectively.

The Hero's Journey pattern is so refined in filmmaking that people give an enormous amount of attention to precisely when any piece of this pattern should take place to have the highest possible impact. You can feel when it's right. It hits a sweet spot the same way as when Louis Armstrong nailed a high note or Michael Jordan sank a jump shot.

But isn't this what's made big, fat Hollywood movies so bad lately? Isn't this what's called "formulaic" and "derivative" by the critics? Isn't this why we have so many movies that seem to deliver the same thing over and over again? No. Randy discussed this, and it's important to underline. Formulaic stories are the result of laziness and fear. Laziness, because it's easier to deliver something generic and familiar. And fear, because the industry is afraid the whole thing will go belly up if it doesn't keep doing just that. That's not Story's fault.

And when we talk about "Hollywood" in this book, it's not just referencing a limited location or system. There exists a tremendously diverse body of work from both studio and independent, domestic and foreign films to show us what works.

The pattern is elegant, strong, and flexible. The pattern can look so many different ways that we've made movies for over a century without most people realizing that it's all the same story.

Ripley in *Alien* is the same character as Sam Spade in *The Maltese Falcon*, who is the same character as King George in *The King's Speech*.

Doesn't that seem absurd and yet somehow totally intuitive?

And with smart storytelling, a professor on trial in Missouri, an engineer researching bionics in Texas, and a police detective trying to solve a case in Massachusetts can also be the same character as Ripley, Sam, and George.

Most likely, once you've gotten to know the principles laid out in this book, you'll start to see this pattern everywhere. The Hero's Journey will rise up before you, and suddenly, you'll see it in the movie you're watching, the book you're reading...the life you're living.

The great news is if you can see it, you can make it.

IT'S AS EASY AS ONE, TWO, THREE

And, But, and Therefore. I love that this is the pattern as Randy has recognized it, because it just doesn't get any simpler. I'm going to make it a little bit more complex for you. I'm going to help you figure out what goes between the "and, but, and therefore."

The most primary element of Story is that it happens in three distinct parts, like the "and, but, and therefore." This also shows up in structure as "thesis, antithesis, and synthesis," Hegel's "bud, flower, fruit," or just plain old "beginning, middle, and end." Which is great, because most people, natural storytellers or not, understand the concept of beginning, middle, and end.

The second most important element of Story is the "Hero," also called the "Protagonist." The hero is who, or what, the story is centered around. The hero is the one who wants something, the one who does something about getting it, and the one who achieves it.

See? Beginning, middle, and end again.

So here we have two things: On one hand, we have a heroic figure. On the other hand, we have a story in three parts. If you take a hero, and put that hero on the three-part road of the "and, but, and therefore," you have a story.

Is it really that easy? Actually, yes. We'll take a deeper look later, but here, at the threshold of becoming a storyteller, let's just see how basic this really can be.

THE BEGINNING

"In the beginning..." "Once up a time..." "In a world where..."

These are pretty well known openings, right? That's because before we do anything else, we have to establish what's going on already.

In the pro-Obama ad, Mike Earnest expresses this as "Out of the blue one day..."

In Campbell's Monomyth, this is called "The Ordinary World." More on this later, but for now, we can just go with the fact that it's actually pretty ordinary...to the hero. Maybe not at all to the average human. The hero and their world are in a state of stasis: nothing really wrong, but maybe nothing really right either.

The "but" also happens here in the beginning section. As Randy says, "A story starts when something happens." In Monomyth parlance, this is called "The Call to Adventure." What happens is that the hero is called to go on a journey (physical or conceptual), or someone or something enters the ordinary world that demands a response from the hero.

The beginning of the story is the thesis, because the premise and theme of the story are introduced. We learn here what the hero's major goal and major challenge will be.

This is where we ask: "What if...?"

THE MIDDLE

In the Monomyth, this is called "The Special World." This is because in many ways it's the opposite of the ordinary world. This is also why it's the antithesis. The hero sees things in a whole new light.

This may or may not be a different physical space from where the hero was when the story began, but the hero does cross a "threshold." It's different emotionally, psychologically, and the hero has a new, highly focused intention.

In the middle of the story, the hero directly pursues their goal and battles the forces of conflict to achieve it.

For a while, the hero makes good progress towards their goal, but then conflict starts to win. The hero has to dig deep and learn what they have to learn in order to get what they want.

Finally, they're ready to face the conflict.

THE END

This is the climax of the story. This is where the hero wins. This is also called the synthesis, because in Monomyth language, the hero becomes "The Master of Two Worlds," as they incorporate the best of everything that they've learned to achieve their desired goal.

Now we have resolution, and the story comes to an end. The hero has accepted the call to change their world, and they have changed it.

ONCE UPON AN A.B.T.

Once Upon a Time...the hero is in their ordinary world AND they feel that they understand it very well.

BUT a call to adventure changes everything, and creates a goal the hero wants to achieve more than anything.

THEREFORE the hero heads out on the journey into a special world to get what they want, and in spite of the conflict working against them, the hero prevails.

The End.

That's a story. That's every story.

The Monomyth is at the core of every great story. The structure is universal. It connects.

HOLLYWOOD? REALLY?

Most people think of "Hollywood" as being very different from them in nearly every way. When I first met my man's family, some of them were a little standoffish with me. These are all decent, hard-working, blue-collar folks from rural New York. To them I *was* Hollywood, which meant I was probably a narcissistic druggie who couldn't do single-digit addition in my head. I understand that. Hollywood gets a bad rap. "But enough about me...what do you think about me?"

I'm just asking you to set aside whatever negative notions about Hollywood you might have and just look at the structure that exists as the building blocks of our stories. Because, you know what? Hollywood stories work. The structure works. They connect to a huge cross-section of the population.

Whatever my new family thought of me at first, it wasn't long before we were all happily talking about how funny the latest Steve Carell movie was. Whatever you perceive about the ethics of the culture, the proof of the effectiveness of its product is in its massive appeal. You may distrust Hollywood, but it's a treasure trove of storytelling tools.

And we all get Steve Carell. That kind of connection is as good as gold.

NOW WHAT ABOUT YOU?

L et's take a look at what Story can look like in your world. How can Hollywood help in the courtroom? The classroom? The lab? The museum? The bedside of a hospice patient? The village that needs to learn the vital importance of clean water and how to get it?

No matter who you are, no matter what your story is, no matter who you want to affect and what you hope they'll do…it's all the same story.

FACT OR FICTION?

N ow, most of you are not in the storytelling business. Or maybe you are. But the biggest thing we need to look at before going any farther is a question we hear a lot: Does my story need to be true? Or does it need to be made up?

If you have a fact-based story you want to tell, then you must stick to the absolute truth. But if you feel like diving into fiction, and it's appropriate to your needs, you can invent a story. As long as you're completely upfront with your audience about which form it is you're telling—fact or fiction—there are myriad applications for both.

Telling a fictional story may or may not be right for your final purposes, but learning how to *create* one is invaluable practice. If what you ultimately need to deliver needs to be true, that's fine; you'll get there. But if you have to take a brief detour and get your feet wet on a story about a hitchhiking pig who desperately wants to study fashion design, go for it.

WHAT CAN WE LEARN FROM FACT?

It doesn't matter if it's fact or fiction; the "rules" of narrative are the same. What's going to be most different is how you find, identify, and choose your material.

If your story is fact, you're going to be culling from the information and research available around you. You're going to be looking into the real-life history of your tech start-up company or an epidemic outbreak. It could be the homecoming of a particular soldier from the Middle East, the discovery that the age of the universe is different than we thought, the personal biography of a defendant in a lawsuit. Telling a true story is going to be a matter of learning the traditional story elements, then learning how to identify them in the verifiable reality around you so you can use them factually and effectively. The concept of Story does not imply fiction, nor does it suggest permission to invent if your audience believes what they're hearing is true.

Fact is also powerful when "truth is stranger than fiction." What this can mean for you—crafting your story from the facts—is that you might discover that you have at your disposal an element from reality that's so amazing it could never meet its rival in the imagination. As Brian will talk about in his section of this book, making this reach an audience is going to be all about how you tell it.

Stephen Colbert brought a great amount of attention to a video, made by National Geographic and the Monterey Bay Aquarium Research Institute, by making fun of the video's soporific voice narration. The moving image is of a stunning barrel-eye fish that has bright green tubular eyes encased in a see-through head. While NatGeo's calm narration explains in a rather tepid way how the fish sees, in Colbert's world, this is one of the "Craziest F#?ng Things I've Ever Heard!!" The hits on the original video leaped to what is now well over 4 million.

WHAT CAN WE LEARN FROM FICTION?

"You know what your problem is? It's that you haven't seen enough movies. All of life's riddles are answered in the movies"
— Davis in *Grand Canyon*: 1991, screenplay by Lawrence Kasdan and Meg Kasdan

Most of us have more common experience with fictional stories. Yes, most of us have studied some history and have access to the news, but not all of us spend time getting emotionally invested or following the whole story. Or we might be following the news stories on different formats, with different points of view and biases. As for most of our own factual stories, no one outside our intimate circles will ever know.

But you and I might both know exactly how Carrie and Brody first got together on *Homeland*.

Thanks to modern technology, we can all watch and get to know the exact same fictional stories. There's a fairly good chance of you having seen, or being able to see, one of the movies mentioned in this book. If we're using *Alien* as a case study, there's a better chance of you getting exactly what I'm talking about than if I refer to that time in my family where everyone was all heated up over what to do with Grandma's diamond necklace. But if you haven't seen *Alien*, by all means do. Grandma's necklace didn't have metal-dissolving saliva as a defense mechanism. Much more exciting.

Fiction can have a way of elevating and crystallizing emotion for learning purposes that doesn't always show up as neatly or obviously in non-fiction formats. Fiction—although no better than fact—has a way of highlighting the emotional elements of story in a way that makes it very easy to see and to understand.

Whether you prefer Judd Apatow or the History Channel, watching stories, looking for the patterns of structure, studying how they're organized, and seeing what they reveal about the depth and wonder of human nature, are going to be immeasurably fruitful for you in learning how to craft your own story.

HYPOTHETICALLY SPEAKING...

Either fact or fiction can be effective in any number of circumstances, as long as your audience knows which kind of story you're telling. When it's fact, we stick to the facts. When it's fiction, we let that be known.

Hypothetically speaking, some of you might use an allegorical tale as a way of warming up your audience before you deliver a more substantive speech, hooking their attention with a fictive situation similar to what your data describes. Some of you might use a fable to help a prospective donor envision what it might feel like to fund an outreach program. Some of you might use historical fiction to demonstrate to your students what it would have been like to live in another time and place.

For most of you, the most common use of fiction will likely be a hypothetical story. This is a way of using fiction to illustrate a point that captures the audience's imagination and connects them to the subject emotionally. Again, this is not an excuse or permission to invent if the audience has been led to believe that the story is true, but an openly stated hypothetical can create an environment where people can engage as if it could be true, even just for that moment.

Many of you will never use the option of fiction, sticking purely to the facts you need to tell. But for those of you with the freedom to invent to help inspire and imagine, using fiction can be a wonderful way of asking "what if...?"

TOLSTOY'S TWO STORIES

There's a lot of debate about how many possible plots actually exist. Some say there are seven. Thirty-six is a popular number. There are love stories. Coming of age stories. One-last-chance stories. There are crime stories. Drama. Science fiction and science fact. There are happy-ending stories that lift us up. Tragic stories that teach us a tough lesson.

But in a way, all these genres and plots are really just a matter of style. It's not that details don't matter. Specifics are what stories are made of.

Leo Tolstoy, the beloved Russian author of *War and Peace*, said it best. "There are only two stories: A man goes on a journey, or a stranger comes to town."

If you can take your ideas, facts, research, and concepts and build them around one of those two "plots," you've got yourself a story.

Now let's find out how to do that.

PART TWO: THIS IS LOGLINE

Let me tell you a story...

A talented but arrogant out-of-work actor, desperate for acknowledgement, auditions for a soap opera disguised as a woman and gets the part, finding instant popularity. But when he falls in love with his female co-star and receives a marriage proposal from her father, he has to learn to be as good a man as he is a woman, so he can earn love, respect—and work—as himself.
— *Tootsie*: 1982, screenplay by Larry Gelbart

How about another one?

When a spoiled young woman's husband dies on their wedding night, she joins the Army to forget herself, and after an embattled beginning, she thrives. But when she falls in love again with an unfaithful man who tries to control her, she has to remember what strong stuff she's really made of before she loses her chance to truly live.
— *Private Benjamin*: 1980, screenplay by Nancy Meyers & Charles Shyer

Here in Hollywood, stories come in different sizes. But every Hollywood story, whether it's a commercial or a long-running television series, has at the heart of it something called the Logline. The Logline is simply the shortest, most efficient and elegant way of stating what the story is.

The Logline is the distillation of the entire classical Hero's Journey into just a sentence or two, like the stories written above. This is what you're going learn how to make. This is Logline. This is Story.

While both the above stories are fiction, the structure is going to be the same for a story that's based on fact. It might not be as fanciful as *Tootsie*, but *Private Benjamin* is within the realm of possibility.

This might seem daunting at first, but it's just an expansion of the "and, but, and therefore" theory with some extra steps to build it up. The structure of the Logline is like the framework of a house; it gives you something to build on.

Here are two great things to get you excited about writing your Logline:

1) *Once you've written the Logline, you have a complete story.*

The Logline is a perfectly constructed, easy-to-tell story. On one hand, the Logline is a plan for a longer, more fleshed-out story. And on the other hand, it's a complete story. However you want to use it, once you've crafted it, you're ready to go.

2) *The Logline is very satisfying to create.*

When you're writing a story, fact or fiction, it feels great to roll up your sleeves and get into it. You work it; rework it. You love your story; you hate your story. You cry a little, have too much coffee, go shopping for something you don't really need, start writing again...and come out the other side with something that's ready to tell and ready to connect with an audience.

Okay, there probably won't be tears. There might be coffee. I'm not here to tell you that crafting great stories is always easy. Making stories is creating, and creating takes energy. Getting into the emotions of the story, and how it makes you feel to write it, is all part of the picture.

Enjoy writing the Logline. Play around with it. You'll feel a little more alive right after you make your first great story. Stories are not just persuasive communication; they're very satisfying.

A SHIFT

A police chief, afraid of the water, has just transferred to an island of narrow-minded xenophobes when a teenage girl's body is found ravaged by a predatory shark. The chief tries to close the beaches, angering the town, which wants to preserve summer tourism. But when the shark eats a young boy, the chief, along with a pretentious young scientist and an abrasive old mariner, goes to sea to hunt down and kill the rogue shark before it can murder anyone else.

— *Jaws*: 1975, screenplay by Peter Benchley and Carl Gottlieb

All truly great stories are about heroes making a big shift in their lives by taking on something way outside their comfort zone. In *Jaws*, Chief Brody deeply fears the water, but that's the only place he can go if he wants to kill the shark.

For many of you, creating a story is going to be way outside your comfort zone. And like in many stories, the biggest reward often comes to those who are most reluctant. Going from not knowing what a story is made of, or not wanting to know, or being outright hostile to the idea...going from that to telling a well-structured, relatable, and emotionally effective story is a powerful shift.

If you give it a shot and embrace the structure, the Logline Maker can give you not only great skills and techniques, but also the feeling of what it's like to really know Story. And the feeling of being able to tell a story and feel it connect with the people hearing it—there's no other feeling quite like it in the world.

What is the Logline Maker? Well...

FILL IN THE BLANKS

The Logline Maker is a game of Fill-in-the-**BLANKS**. Each **BLANK** is a separate element of Story with a specific meaning. Some might seem familiar right off the bat, and some might not. I'm going to explain them all to you. By the time we've worked through a few more of these stories, it'll start to feel familiar. You'll have some nice "ah ha" moments next time you're watching a movie, or reading a book, or checking out the news. These elements are all around you. Once you know them, you'll be able to recognize them in stories you see and hear.

And if you follow this structure, filling in the **BLANKS** with as much specificity and emotional depth as possible, you'll have a story that connects effectively with a wide number of people.

The **BLANKS** in the Logline Maker and the order in which they happen are what make the story universal. These **BLANKS** happen in all good stories, everywhere. They are in Shakespeare and in the films of Quentin Tarantino.

How you decide to fill in the **BLANKS** is what makes your story specific to you and what you want to say.

It'll be fun. Here we go.

THE LOGLINE MAKER

Here is the elegant, innate structure of Story:

1. **IN AN ORDINARY WORLD...**
2. **A FLAWED PROTAGONIST** gets **HER/HIS/ THEIR**
   life upended when
3. **A CATALYTIC EVENT HAPPENS**.
4. After **TAKING STOCK**,
5. **THE HERO COMMITS TO ACTION**.
6. But when **THE STAKES GET RAISED**
7. **THE HERO MUST LEARN THE LESSON**
8. in order to **STOP THE ANTAGONIST,**
9. so **THE HERO CAN ACHIEVE THEIR GOAL**.

Or in a more natural, storytelling style:

In an ordinary world...a flawed protagonist gets their life upended when a catalytic event happens. After taking stock, the hero commits to action. But when the stakes get raised, the hero must learn the lesson in order to stop the antagonist, so the hero can achieve their goal.

That sounds like a story doesn't it? That's what a story is.

STORY #1

Here's an example with the BLANKS filled in:

1. **IN A TIME OF A GALACTIC CIVIL WAR, ON A QUIET FARM...**

2. **AN IMPATIENT YOUNG MAN** gets **HIS** life upended when

3. **HE FINDS A MESSAGE FROM A KIDNAPPED PRINCESS AND MEETS AN OLD MAN WHO TELLS HIM ABOUT "THE FORCE."**

4. After **HIS FAMILY IS MURDERED,**

5. **THE YOUNG MAN HIRES A COCKY SPACE PILOT TO HELP HIM RESCUE THE PRINCESS AND AID THE REBEL ALLIANCE.**

6. But when **THE PRINCESS' HOME PLANET IS DESTROYED AND THE YOUNG MAN IS DRAWN INTO THE ENEMY'S BATTLE STATION,**

7. **HE MUST LEARN HOW TO USE "THE FORCE"**

8. in order to **DESTROY THE ENEMY,**

9. so **HE CAN SAVE THE PRINCESS AND THE REBEL ALLIANCE.**

It can be hard to "hear" the story like that, but it's much easier like this:

In a time of galactic civil war, on a quiet farm...an impatient young man gets his life upended when he finds a message from a kidnapped princess and meets an old man

who tells him about "The Force." After his family is murdered, the young man hires a cocky space pilot to help him rescue the princess and aid the Rebel Alliance. But when the princess' home planet is destroyed and the young man is drawn into the enemy's battle station, he must learn how to use "The Force" in order to destroy the enemy, and save the princess and the Rebel Alliance.

Doesn't that sound like a good story? It's *Star Wars*, written in 1977 by George Lucas.

Star Wars is not only one of the most famous, beloved films ever made, but it's credited with bringing awareness of Joseph Campbell's *Hero of a Thousand Faces* to the Hollywood forefront via filmmaker George Lucas, who carefully crafted the first *Stars Wars* film after the Hero's Journey. He closely followed the structure of the Monomyth, delivering an enduringly powerful story that uses familiar elements from multiple mythologies, but in a unique and specific fashion. More than thirty-five years later, this story is still resonant, exciting, and relevant. It's universally appealing in great part because it follows the pattern right down the line. Lucas was highly creative and detailed in how he filled in each of the **BLANKS**, but it's no different than what you're going to do with your story. Because it's the same story.

Let's do it again:

STORY #2

1.   **IN THE MACHO WORLD OF WALL STREET...**

2.   **TESS, A SMART BUT UNREFINED SECRETARY FROM STATEN ISLAND**, gets **HER** life upended when

3. **SHE'S HIRED BY AN EGOTISTICAL EXECU-TIVE, CATHERINE, WHO PRETENDS TO SUPPORT HER BUT IS ACTUALLY STEALING HER IDEAS.**

4. After **CATHERINE GOES TO EUROPE ON VACATION LEAVING TESS IN CHARGE,**

5. **TESS TAKES OVER HER LIFE, PRETENDS TO BE AN EXECUTIVE, AND TURNS ONE OF HER OWN IDEAS INTO A LUCRATIVE DEAL.**

6. But when **CATHERINE COMES HOME EARLY AND REVEALS TO EVERYONE WHO TESS REALLY IS,**

7. **TESS MUST OWN UP TO HOW SMART SHE IS EVEN WITHOUT THE DISGUISE**

8. in order to **STOP CATHERINE FROM CLAIM-ING OWNERSHIP OF HER IDEA,**

9. so **TESS CAN BE TAKEN SERIOUSLY ON WALL STREET.**

And this way:

In the macho world of Wall Street…Tess, a smart but unre-fined sec- retary from Staten Island, gets her life upended when she's hired by an egotistical executive, Catherine, who pretends to support her but is actually stealing her ideas. After Catherine goes to Europe on vacation leaving Tess in charge, Tess takes over her life, pretends to be an executive, and turns one of her own ideas into a lucrative deal. But when Catherine comes home early and reveals to everyone who Tess really is, Tess must own up to how

smart she is, even without the disguise, in order to stop Catherine from claiming ownership of her idea, so Tess can be taken seriously on Wall Street.

This is *Working Girl*, written in 1988 by Kevin Wade. It's a terrific movie, starring the luminous yet accessible Melanie Griffith. The hero has a clear external goal, a terrific transformation, and the story provides a satisfyingly emotional pay-off.

I've written the Logline a little differently in this version. The protagonist and the antagonist have both been given proper names, Tess and Catherine. Look at what a difference that makes. They become more alive. A personality comes into focus. All in a name. That's pretty powerful.

Take another look at the two Loglines we worked out here. Read them through out loud. See how easy it is to tell a story that's been crafted so efficiently. That's why this pattern has been around for so long and why Story is the single best way to tell people something you really want them to hear.

Story is the spoonful of sugar that makes the medicine go down. But structure is the spoon.

THE POWER OF A NAME

A woman in our workshop was working on a story. It was fine. She had a hero, they wanted something, there was conflict. But it wasn't really connecting emotionally with the group. We were debating about what was going on when Randy said, "Your hero. What's the guy's name?"

She said, "I don't know. I never thought about it. Um...Paul."

She read the story through again exactly with the same wording as before, but now she called the hero of her story "Paul." Suddenly it clicked. You could feel it in the room, like goose bumps. Everyone got it at once. Whereas "the microbiologist" wasn't catching our attention, we really got into the story about

"Paul." We felt like we knew him, we wanted him to do well, and when he succeeded, we felt happy.

When you need your hero to make an impression, give them a name.

It's a terrific example that the smallest possible detail about someone can suddenly make them come to life. A well-chosen name can be the first way to tell your listeners that your story is about someone that really matters.

BREAKING IT DOWN

Looking at Story as one big problem to solve is overwhelming. But in the next part we're going to talk about what each of the **BLANKS** in the Logline Maker is all about. We're going to break it down.

Say one morning you go out to your car, ready to take the kids to school, drive to work, then pick up dinner...and you discover that your car won't start. It's going to be a very difficult day if you feel that suddenly your whole day is a problem. But if you break the problem down into smaller chunks, it's a much easier task to take on. That's why the Logline makes crafting a story so much easier. It gets broken down into parts.

Some of your Logline elements will be easy to identify and choose. Maybe you already know who you want your story to be about. It's about your organization. Or a historical figure. Or a personal hero of yours. Maybe it's about a fictional character based on an amalgamation of different people you know. Maybe you know what the goal is. Maybe you know exactly how they go about accomplishing that. You might know the conflict or the antagonist. That's great. Those pieces are in place.

But maybe you don't know something. Or maybe you don't know anything yet. Maybe you're looking at a blank sheet of paper or at your computer cursor just blinking at you. What are you supposed to do then?

Look at it piece by piece. Start breaking it down.

MAKING CHOICES

There are no wrong choices. You cannot make a mistake. I'm not just saying that to be encouraging and inclusive. It's just true.

There's no way you can choose something that is wrong. A choice might have less impact than it could. There might be a choice that leads you down a path that's more confusing than it needs to be. That's fine. It's a process. You're also going to make choices that are great, choices that can open up a whole new world of possibility.

Choices aren't just for fiction. Choices apply to fact as well. When crafting non-fiction, you'll make choices about how to best make use of the facts...all within the strict bounds of reality.

Don't worry if you make a choice that has to get changed later. That's just writing.

The structure is there; you just need to keep building.

BE SPECIFIC

There's a great adage here in the story business: The Specific is the Universal. In plain language, this means that the more specific something is—the more personal and real it is—the bigger chance you have of connecting with the most people.

This might sound odd, even counterintuitive. But sometimes we feel like we have to cast a wide net to make our stories universally appealing. Instead of going wide, go small. Think details. This doesn't mean a huge amount of data, but carefully chosen, meaningful pieces of information that help us understand the hero and their story.

Because we're specific and unique, and we're human, when we see something else specific and unique, we all point and sigh, "Ah! That's what it's like to be human. That's what it's like to be me."

That's why stories connect.

130   CONNECTION

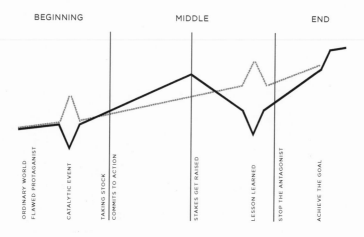

FIGURE 8 - THE LOGLINE. *The nine elements of the Logline are shown as they happen over the course of the story, in relation to the Hero's Progress and level of Conflict.*

PART THREE: THE ELEMENTS

Okay, you ready? We're going to break these elements on down.

ELEMENT #1: IN AN ORDINARY WORLD...

I'm in a dark movie theatre, happily seated in time for the previews. Booming over the sound system is a deep bass voice saying "In world where..." and I'm already excited. They just told me that I'm about to hear a story.

And with this moment, we've arrived at our first decision to make: In what world does this story begin?

The ordinary world is the world that is ordinary to the hero. It's a place where the hero is (at least relatively) comfortable. They understand the world. The hero may feel very powerful in that world. They may hope that the world never changes. They know the rules and how to get by. They know what their status is in that world, and have come to accept it. For now.

Often, the ordinary world is a place of stagnation. There's something about the world that has reached a tipping point where if it doesn't grow, it will die. The ordinary world isn't just literal; it's also a metaphor for the internal place the hero is in when the story begins. If the hero doesn't grow, they will "die."

The ordinary world of the film *Chinatown* is Los Angeles, 1937, when the population explosion has created a situation where the city can't sustain itself if it doesn't get more water. So they steal it.

Lastly, the ordinary world exists in order to provide a contrast. When we start our stories with "In a world where..." we're establishing how things are in order to be able to fully appreciate what they become.

Your "ordinary world" might be:

- A hospital that hasn't yet taken a close look at the correlation between various nutritional options for patients and the speed of their recovery.
- Two neighbors who don't realize that they each have a very different opinion about where their property line is.
- A state park in which the wildlife tracking system hasn't been updated since the 1980s.

STORY-FISHING

We're going to take a little sidebar and talk about something I like to call "story-fishing."

When telling factual stories, finding story elements to choose from means getting good at figuring out how to find the strongest existing elements within the reality you're dealing with. You need to know what makes a good story, find it, and hook it. How do you do that? To learn how to make choices and to have choices to choose from, you've got to go story-fishing.

My man is a fly-fisherman. I am not. Our very first quarrel as a couple was over me unwittingly horning in on his perfect fishing hole on a river in Montana. He generously led me further down river. Over that week, strapped up in my waders and felt-bottom boots, I learned a few things about fishing.

- The most important thing is patience. You can't rush fishing.
- But you can put yourself where and when it's most likely to happen.
- Know the signs for where the fish are.
- Learn what fish like to eat, and make your fly look like that.

Story-fishing, looking for real-life stories in the world, is the same thing. You get to know what makes a story, where to look, how to dig a little deeper, and soon, you'll become adept at story-fishing. You need patience, knowledge, and a feel for where the fish are. A sense of humor never hurts. And maybe a beer or two.

And for the record, I've caught exactly one fish. A cute little brown trout. Mission accomplished; I was done.

ELEMENT #2: A FLAWED PROTAGONIST

Whose story is this? The protagonist, or hero, is the person in your story who does the most, wants the most, tries the hardest, learns the greatest lesson, and when the hero wins, we win.

Who's your hero? It is a person? Are they like you? Someone you know? Or it could be a turtle looking for a safe place to lay her eggs. We've consulted on a video starring a rather intrepid "Flat Stanley." You never know.

GROUP HEROES

There are companies, armies, schools, cities, and families to tell stories about. This can, and does, absolutely work.

That being said, it's still going to help make the point of the story clearer if one person from the group can take action, learn, and succeed in a way that stands out, that benefits the entire group. This makes it specific.

When looking at your own group story, fact or fiction, is there one person in the group that had something special at stake? Someone that went beyond the bounds of what was expected of them? Even within a larger group, it's effective to focus on one relatable person.

MULTIPLE INDIVIDUAL HEROES

There is also a way to craft a story with multiple individual heroes, though this is a bit more challenging, as each of these heroes will need a complete story of their own. Documentary films are often terrific examples of multiple individual heroes and how fruitful "story-fishing" can be.

Harlon County, U.S.A., made in 1976 by Barbara Kopple, is a powerfully intimate view of coal miners and their families, and one of the best known and most respected documentaries ever made.

When looking at multiple individual heroes, what do they all experience in their own unique way that tells the same basic theme? How does each individual person specifically symbolize the universal theme of the story?

WHAT MAKES FOR A GREAT HERO?

There are infinite ways to be a hero. Don't be limited by thinking that a hero can only be a certain type. It might not even be human. Pixar, one of the modern genius collectives of storytelling, has shown us the enduring compassionate power of the hero toy, fish, truck, rat, and robot.

But there are qualities that we tend to really like in our heroes. Knowing these and using them is to your advantage, so why not?

We tend to like our heroes:

- **Smart:** This doesn't necessarily mean a high IQ, but it can. Good instincts and quick thinking are a good match with the Heroic.
- **Funny:** Giving the hero a great sense of humor is a terrific way to get people emotionally attached to them.
- **Good at what they do:** This is shorthand for a lot of other qualities that are also likable, like hard work, focus, drive, passion, commitment to excellence, and talent.

2. NARRATIVE: HEROES OF HOLLYWOOD

- **Working class**: There's something about really having to work hard at something that makes heroes feel authentic. While a white-collar hero, or even a celebrity, can also be effective, the commitment of mind and body is something we admire.
- **Independent**: We're drawn to people who make things happen without the construct of a larger system supporting them. We tend to admire the impassioned rebels and the freethinkers...within reason.
- **Resilient**: A hero that is willing to roll with the punches and keep on trying is going to get our vote. Harrison Ford has built his whole career around this quality. This sturdiness is also tied to self-sufficiency and optimism.
- **Adaptable**: Many stories are about people who are going through a major life change. Their act of heroism is to be able to come out better for it.

SOMETHING TO LEARN

Okay, now what about this flaw, in the FLAWED PROTAGONIST? Why does there need to be a flaw?

This flaw is actually one of the main things that helps us like our heroes. It's what makes them human, just like us. What the hero has to learn, how they grow and adapt, is what gives the story real meaning. It tells us not just what happens, but what it means for it to happen.

The flaw, or weakness, is something in the hero that needs to be fixed, mastered, or released. This is the Lesson that the hero will learn later. But the idea of it starts here.

DIE HARD: A LOVE STORY

L et's take a look at the movie *Die Hard*. The hero is smart, funny, and good at what he does. He's working class, independent, and resilient. He's got major flaws, but we love him anyway, because no one tries harder than him to make up for it.

Arriving in Los Angeles on Christmas Eve...John McClane, a stubborn, recently separated, New York cop, gets his life upended when a group of thieves takes over his wife's office building. After trying unsuccessfully to get help from the police, McClane decides to handle the situation himself and take down the bad guys. But when the leader of the thieves, Hans, kidnaps his wife, McClane must learn to let go of his stubborn pride in order to stop Hans from getting away with the robbery, so he can save his wife.

John McClane is stingy with his emotions and his apologies. His flaw is that he needs to let go of his pride and support his wife. *Die Hard* looks like a great big action movie, but it's a love story at heart. There's something at the heart of your story, too. Finding it is an important key to the rest of the story.

WHAT'S A USEFUL FLAW?

Here's a short list of some useful flaws:

- Resistance to change
- Fear of getting attached
- Being overly cerebral
- The need to control
- Apathy
- Hubris

Any of these flaws, and those like it, can work wonderfully. None of them are insurmountable, and any of them allows us to still love the hero. Not in spite of them, but because of them. It makes them more like us.

A DIFFERENT KIND OF FLAW

There is another kind of flaw that can be equally effective. In this alternative way of looking at it, there is nothing "wrong" with the hero; they just need to learn a new way of doing things. They might need to learn to:

- Convince
- Collaborate
- Cooperate
- Compromise

Single, group, or multiple hero, fact or fiction...your protagonist learning to do any of these things can be a terrific way of demonstrating growth.

THE MORAL OF THE STORY IS...

This flaw, this lesson, is one of the main reasons we tell stories and get so much out of hearing them. We learn, and feel, the moral of the story.

By structuring the story and crafting the hero in the way it's shown here, the audience will emotionally "become" the hero, flaws, goals, successes, and all. This is the magic of storytelling; done well, it's a truly transformative experience.

Your "flawed protagonist" might be:

- A brilliant young doctor who assumes a certain symptom consistently indicates a certain underlying condition.

- A dedicated teacher who wants the best for her students but has been doing things the same way for twenty years.
- A type-A lobbyist who needs to learn to trust his co-workers to really get things done.

ELEMENT #3: A CATALYTIC EVENT

It happens to everyone. All humans know the experience of something occurring that radically changes everything. And when this happens in a story, people want to know more. This is Randy's "a story starts when something happens" in action. This is the "call to adventure" from Joseph Campbell's Monomyth.

The catalytic event in your story might be a terrible shock, like a massively destructive earthquake. It can be a positive shock, like finding out you just won the party nomination.

This moment is often when the hero first meets their opponent: the antagonist. Whether that antagonist is a person, a disease, or a storm, it's going to create a great amount of conflict. That's a very good thing for your story.

The catalytic event is also the thing that creates or introduces the goal in the hero's mind. Whatever happens here is what makes the hero wake up and realize that they want something.

THE ENEMY AT THE GATE

This story has a marvelous catalytic event: the entrance of Eve, the antagonist.

In the glamorous world of Broadway...Margo Channing, a beloved but aging star, is approached backstage by the young Eve Harrington, Margo's biggest fan. Before long, Eve insidiously inserts herself into Margo's life, even getting cast as her understudy. Margo tries to get her friends to see that Eve is not the innocent she pretends to be, but they dismiss her, thinking she's just jealous. But when

Eve's snide attitude toward Margo is revealed, her friends rally around her. Eve, friendless, is enslaved by her own lust for fame, while Margo joyfully embraces a new life, playing only the roles she wants to.
— *All About Eve*: 1950, screenplay by Joseph L. Mankiewicz

Your "catalytic event" might be:

- The sudden presence of a dangerous invasive species into a fragile environment.
- A new tax law that greatly alters the financial structuring of your organization.
- The arrival of a new CEO who is convinced that a clean sweep of the employees is the best way to go.

ELEMENT #4: AFTER TAKING STOCK

A couple of years ago, when I found out for the second time in as many months that one of my parents had cancer, my very first response was to yell, "That's bullshit!" My mind just totally rejected the idea. Plus, it made me feel better to yell a little.

That's what this section of the story is all about: the hero tries to do anything but accept the full significance of the catalytic event. They take stock, check out their options, weigh the odds. But at the same time, the options are closing, forcing them to move forward. It's best if the hero decides for themselves to pull their head out of the sand and commit to a new goal, but sometimes we all need a little kick in the pants.

By first saying "no" to the call to adventure, saying "yes" later will have a lot more power. Fiction or fact, this moment has the potential to be incredibly human. It's the first part of the story that takes some serious guts.

SOMETIMES YOU GOTTA FIGHT

In *High Noon*, Will Cane has just retired as marshal of a small town and married Amy Fowler, a devout Quaker. As they're about to leave on their honeymoon, Will finds out that Frank Miller, a dangerous criminal that Will put behind bars, is out of prison and heading into town on the noon train.

Will immediately jumps into his horse-drawn carriage with Amy and drives right out of town. But...slowing down, Will realizes that he's just not that kind of man. Retired or not, married or not, he has to stand up to this man. So...he turns around and goes back to town. It's a stirring moment as the hero first rejects the call to adventure, then taking stock, remembers who he really is. It doesn't get any clearer than that.

Your moment of "taking stock" might be:

- Hoping the standardized test scores were an anomaly but getting the same results back the second time.
- Doubting the storm will be as bad as predicted and, at first, deciding to not issue a warning.
- Exhausting every known option of curing a patient before accepting that a totally new path of treatment is going to be required.

ELEMENT #5: THE HERO COMMITS TO ACTION

In the Monomyth, we are now crossing over a "Threshold." In order to get what the hero wants, they must enter the Special World. Sometimes this is literally a new place; other times it's more theoretical. The special world is special because it's new, strange, and comes with a set of rules that are quite different from those that worked in the ordinary world.

The first thing the hero does is learn how this new world works. What the rules are. What they can and can't do. They make new friends who can help them achieve their goal. Build new skills. Strengthen old ones. They have to adapt in order to survive.

Superhero "origin" stories do this particularly well. Spider-man. Batman. When the change happens and they become someone new, they adapt.

GOING FOR THE GOLD

This section of the story is about the commitment to action and the carrying out of that action in pursuit of a specific goal.

The more visual, tangible, measurable, and visceral the goal is, the better the story will work. This is one of the reasons why *Raiders of the Lost Ark* worked so well. Nothing like a great big, shiny, gold Ark of the Covenant holding the remains of the actual Ten Commandments to really motivate a person.

To get people engaged emotionally with your story, give them a goal that they can fully picture in their imagination. Seeing is believing, even in the mind's eye.

ADVANCE!

Once the hero commits to action, they make great forward progress, and it seems as though the hero is going to have no trouble achieving their goal.

What's going on internally is confidence building. The hero discovers that through hard work and applied effort they are increasingly capable of achieving their ultimate goal. They feel stronger, smarter, and more prepared for what they need to do. This section, which ends at the midpoint of your story, tradi-tionally goes out on a high note, the peak of the story so far, both emotionally and externally.

Again, the major points of this part of the story are:

- The hero sets a strong, tangible goal.
- The hero enters the Special World, which has a new set of rules.
- The hero adapts by building new skills and making new friends.
- The hero makes strong progress toward accomplishing their goal.

Your "commitment to action" might be:

- The groundskeeper of a golf course decides to make the entire course truly "green" by using nontoxic fertilizer. He gains support from the owners, and begins to test how different formulas work.
- A woman, whose failing café is in a crime-challenged neighborhood, commits to staying open and starts a wave of smart growth. More businesses are encouraged and follow suit.
- The principal of an elementary school chooses to run for public office so she can help implement the changes her school system really needs, and she confidently gets the initial support she needs.

ELEMENT #6: THE STAKES GET RAISED

Randy's made a great case for the durability and flexibility of his And, But, and Therefore template. "But" is conflict. If a story doesn't have it, it's not really a story.

Here, as the stakes get raised, is where the conflict fully shows its face. Here's where the antagonist, the hero's opponent, starts to win.

Conflict defines the hero more clearly than anything else, because their worst qualities are magnified by it and their best qualities are required of it.

ONE STEP FORWARD AND TWO STEPS BACK

As we move ahead, the story turns more troubling. The hero continues to try to attain their goal, but now they're making less and less progress. Conflict rises exponentially.

Finally, at the peak of greatest tension, the antagonist does something that hurts the hero badly. This moment is often played out in fiction as the death of someone especially dear to the hero. The antagonist pinpoints the hero's greatest weakness and exploits it. If there is no actual antagonist, this happens as a result of the overall conflict.

This is a crucial moment in a story. If not for this terrible moment of loss, the hero would never become who they need to be to get what they want.

ALL ALONE

Action movies are the easiest place to watch this section at play externally. In *Predator*, the conflict is extremely high from the moment the team of highly trained soldiers lands in the jungle. As the stakes get raised, every person on the team is killed except the hero, Dutch, and an indigenous woman, Anna, who is spared because she is unarmed. As Anna runs to get help, Dutch is left to fight the monster all alone.

AT THE ALTAR

Romances are especially good at showing how this looks internally. In *The Proposal*, Margaret Tate is demanding, manipulative, and emotionally detached. She blackmails her assistant, Andrew, into accepting her marriage proposal so she can get her green card. The stakes get raised as Margaret falls in love with Andrew, and she realizes that he is a much better person than she is. Her flaws are the real conflict, and she is her own worst enemy.

Your "stakes getting raised" might be:

- A physician's initial findings about a new treatment that seemed potentially successful are now being directly contradicted by another researcher's findings.
- A community's plan for getting city council approval for a public garden is now directly opposed by an alternate plan to build a new apartment building on the same land.
- The big breakthrough in a legal case now appears to be based on falsified evidence, with no corroborating evidence to support it.

CONFLICT / ANTAGONIST

What's the difference between conflict and the antagonist?

When it comes to overall conflict, here are some options:

- Human vs. Human
- Human vs. Nature
- Human vs. Supernatural
- Human vs. Machine/Technology
- Human vs. Themselves

Every story needs a source of conflict. But it does tend to work best when conflict is represented by a specific antagonist. As an example, the conflict might be "nature," and the antagonist might be a specific volcano threatening to explode. The conflict might be "crime," and the antagonist is a specific criminal gang.

Another way to think about it is that the conflict is a certain kind of power, and the antagonist is the person or thing that best represents that power and brings the conflict into sharp focus.

An antagonist can also be a group, the same way there can be a group hero. These can be effective, too. But the reason a single antagonist helps (even if it's an inanimate thing or an approaching event) is that it gives your hero someone/something very specific to be in active conflict with. Putting a "face" on the conflict makes it clear.

The more conflict in a story, the better! The more powerful the forces working against your hero, the better!

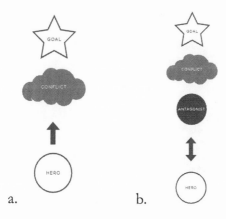

a.   b.

FIGURE 9 – CONFLICT/ANTAGONIST: A) The hero confronts conflict to achieve their goal. B) The hero confronts conflict and an active antagonist to achieve their goal.

WHAT TYPES OF CONFLICT ARE THERE?

There are two types of conflict between a protagonist and an antagonist. They both work, but one tends to work better.

The first type is OFFSET CONFLICT:

- The protagonist wants something.
- The antagonist wants something different.
- They can't both have what they want because they are mutually exclusive.

The second type is DIRECT CONFLICT:

- The protagonist wants something.
- The antagonist wants the exact same thing.
- They can't both have the exact same thing.

Two kids are arguing in the back of a car. One wants to go to Disneyland; the other wants to go to the beach. If Disneyland wins, it's not as major of a loss, as the winner didn't take away the beach, just made it impossible for the moment. But if two kids are arguing over the same tree house, the kid who wins is going to have exactly what the other kid wanted. It's gone forever for one kid. This is what makes the Love Triangle such an enduring story form. It doesn't have to be love that motivates direct conflict, but paying attention to how love triangle stories play out is a good education in how it works.

If the fact or fiction story you're writing seems to be an offset conflict, that's absolutely fine and can work, but consider ways that you can adjust it so that the conflict is more direct. It's going to have the strongest emotional impact.

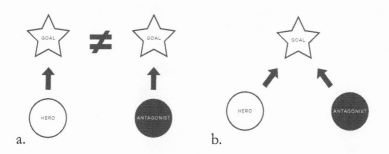

*FIGURE 10 - TWO TYPES OF CONFLICT: A) Offset conflict – the hero and antago-
nist want two mutually exclusive things. B) Direct conflict – the hero and antagonist want the
exact same thing.*

ELEMENT #7: THE HERO MUST LEARN THE LESSON

This is one of those beautiful elements of storytelling where philosophy and practicality unite. Contained within this one section are three stages—death, gestation, and rebirth—which, as a whole, serves a strong function in moving the story forward.

At this point, the conflict has gotten the better of the hero. The hero is knocked down, has to tend to their wounds, and discovers the strength to rise again. They come up with a new plan, and recommit to action.

The rebirth is only possible because of the "death" and retreat. This is Learning the Lesson. The hero must learn to overcome their flaw and come to understand the theme (or lesson) of the whole story. In order to obtain their goal, they need to go through these growing pains, become a complete person, and only then can they accomplish their goal from the best place possible.

Caper movies tend to have a rather clear physical expression of this element, especially when it's a group heist story. Both *Ocean's 11* films have a terrific lesson-learning element.

In a caper film, the stakes are often raised when something unexpected happens that jeopardizes the entire plan, making it seem as though the job must be scrapped. However, everyone pulls together as a team (which is often the lesson in group protagonist stories), they make a strong commitment to the new plan, and plow ahead.

Your hero's "lesson" might be:

- A biologist's persistent attention to the life cycle of an invasive species doesn't explain how the species is getting transported into the environment. *You can't see the forest for the trees.*
- A librarian who's lobbied the school board tirelessly for more books realizes that she's been trying to do everything herself instead of engaging the students and their parents. *Many hands make light work.*
- An anti-piracy lawyer championing musicians' rights discovers that the lawmakers governing the decisions have never personally met a musician. *Put a face on the debate.*

ELEMENT #8: STOP THE ANTAGONIST

And with this, we rocket into the climax of the story, the nail biter of an ending, ready to face the dragon!

Stated simply, "stopping the antagonist" is a very clear thing to describe. Chief Brody kills the shark. Salieri forces Amadeus to write the Requiem for him. Dorothy melts the Wicked Witch.

Whoever your antagonist is, now is when the hero rises up and defeats them, stopping them from carrying out their plan.

"MAKE 'EM LAUGH!"

...unless you're writing a tragedy.

While there is certainly potential for tragic stories to be rather effective teaching tools, there is a strong argument for a happy ending when the purpose is to inspire or encourage further action. People like a happy ending because it makes them happy. That's not as reductive as it sounds, as most of our efforts in life are in the direct pursuit of happiness. Give an audience that feeling, some real reason for optimism and hope, and they'll be much more likely to take that lesson out into the world.

PROVE IT

A life lesson isn't fully learned until it's tested. This is the hero's chance to prove that they are everything they need to be, and know everything they need to know, in order to fully achieve their goal. When they do that, they stop the antagonist.

And with that, there is nothing left—physical or emotional—standing between your hero and what they want. Now all they have to do is take it.

Your "stopping the antagonist" might look like:

- A longtime nurse practitioner, risking her job, reveals unsafe practices in her workplace.
- A third-party outsider candidate, after a grueling race, beats the incumbent in the election for city council.
- A soybean farmer convinces his reluctant county supervisor to allow him to put wind turbines on his property.

ELEMENT #9: THE HERO CAN ACHIEVE THEIR GOAL

In workshops, at the end of the day, we all stand around in a circle and everyone tells their Loglines, which now not only sound like real stories, but *are* real stories. There have been times when I've heard someone's story and actually cried. Not like I just saw *Beaches*, or anything. C'mon, it's a workshop. But it gets me.

The hero has struggled, made friends, built skills, and defeated the antagonist. Now the goal is theirs, and they grasp it. Hooray! The even bigger reason to celebrate is the internal goal being achieved. The hero bravely became the best person they could be. And now they get to feel exactly what they've been hoping to feel all along. The whole goal, everything the hero has been striving for, is not just to hold something in their hand, but for that something to give them a certain feeling. In each story, that's its own special thing.

In 1947...Andy Dufresne, a wealthy banker, is wrongfully convicted of killing his wife and sent to a notoriously harsh prison. After a torturous first few years, Andy realizes he has valuable financial advice to offer and is soon doing the prison accounting, including the warden's personal money laundering. Andy uses his influence to build a prison library and help other inmates get a good education. But when Andy realizes that he's become too crucial to the warden to ever be set free, he escapes through a hole he's secretly been carving for twenty years. He withdraws the warden's pilfered money from the bank, and alerts the newspaper to the prison's abuses before making it safely to a small coastal town in Mexico, a free man.

— *Shawshank Redemption*: 1994, written by Frank Darabont

Whatever we want in life, it's not just the material things. It's not really the car, or the house, or the job that we want, though those are nice to have, too. It's the feeling we get from having those things that we want. The feeling of love, security, freedom, triumph, or hope.

"Remember, Red, hope is a good thing, maybe the best of things. And no good thing ever dies."
— Andy from *Shawshank Redemption*

Your "hero achieving the goal" might be:

- A shipment of a hundred new sewing machines finally arrives so that many impoverished women can now support themselves.
- A new wing of the pediatric care unit in the city hospital opens, and is celebrated with a ribbon-cutting ceremony.
- A rapidly growing company is able to open a factory in another state, opening up jobs for 3000 more workers.

PART FOUR: NOW IT'S YOUR TURN

Well, that was it! All the elements. Now you have the framework in place. The next part is up to you and the story you want to tell.

Most people who are coming to this work for the first time fall into one of two categories. Either this feels pretty natural and makes sense according to their experience, or it feels awful, foreign, and like I just ruined your favorite movie.

I hope it makes sense, but if I just ruined *Harry Potter* for you, I apologize. I'm not the most fun person to watch a movie with.

THE ICEBERG THEORY

So why is there so much to think about when the Logline Maker is just nine short phrases?

The first reason is that the Logline Maker, while a complete story in and of itself, also functions as an overpass of what can be a larger, more fleshed-out story. Eventually, your story can be written in your own style and involve a greater level of specificity than the Logline. There are many details about your story you're going to want to think about when you're still in Logline Maker mode. If you start building it in at the beginning, it's going to be much easier than backtracking to do the work again.

Secondly, the more you know about what each element of Story is about, the smarter choices you can make. Knowing the options, and ways that others have made those choices, helps make your Logline as strong as possible. The more informed decisions that go into your Logline, the higher chance you'll have of crafting an effective story.

Third is something called the Iceberg Theory, an elegant metaphor coined by Ernest Hemingway, the influential American writer, winner of 1954's Nobel Prize in Literature.

Roughly 90 percent of an iceberg's mass is under water, with only 10 percent being visible. In storytelling, that means 90 percent of the work goes into buoying up your story from underneath. This is 90 percent of all the carefully thought-out details that build specificity and emotional authenticity. While the reader or audience might never be consciously aware of these details, they will definitely be aware of the depth supporting the story.

The research you do, the people you interview, the knowledge you bring to every decision about your story…it'll be felt, reinforcing the story we see.

WHY?!

It's only natural for there to be some questions. It can be challenging to learn to build a story the way you'd build a barn.

Let's take a look at a few.

Does it have to be a "Hero"? That sounds so…heroic.

If this word doesn't work for you, that's fine. You can find your own language.

But a Hero does not necessarily have "Here I come to save the day!" qualities. There's a version of the Hero that's just as beloved to people as the Superman version. It's called the Everyman. They aren't especially brave, brilliant, or strong. Not at first. But we see ourselves in this Everyman, this Everyperson, because they're real humans. Their heroism comes from their willingness to put aside their fears and doubts to do what needs to be done, to help others, and to help themselves. Ultimately, the act of bravery required to act like a hero makes them a hero after all.

The 1979 film *Norma Rae* is a perfect example of this. The scene in which she attempts to convince her frustrated husband that she can fight for unionization at her factory and still keep house by demonstrating that she can cook dinner, do the ironing, and make love to him all the same time is pure Everyperson.

Step up to the heroism. It's at the heart of every good story, and it looks as many different ways as there are people in the world.

Where do I start?

Jump on in. Remember that there are no wrong choices.

When creating a fictional hero, start filling in the blanks of who that person might be, what they want, and what they do about it. Some decisions will be fruitful and spark more, new ideas. Some might be a dead end. That's okay. Just turn around and make a new choice.

When identifying a factual hero, look around you—in your company, your organization, people you meet, in the stories you hear—for people who have heroic qualities. Ask questions. People like to tell their stories.

Keep an eye on the stories you see in the world, in the news, in television, even television commercials. Soon, you'll be adept at recognizing the elements of Story. Which means you can find them in the world and use them.

What if my story has a different structure than the Hero's Journey?

Believe it or not, while it's pretty easy to tell a long, unstructured story any old way you want to, it's pretty hard to tell a concise, compelling one in a different structure. Again, it's like a house. Whether it's a Craftsman Bungalow or a Geodesic Dome, if it's got a roof and some walls, you can live in it.

You could spend a lot of time trying to invent a new structure, but this structure has been around for at least two millennia. Why fight it? It works.

Isn't it better to come up with a whole new surprising pattern?

Not really. First of all, see the note about the two thousand years. That's a whole lot of proof that the pattern works.

Secondly, though people do like to be surprised, they also like to be rewarded. For example, audiences emotionally crave the sensation of seeing the hero rise up again after getting beaten down by the antagonist. Giving it to them is rewarding.

Won't people just be expecting the ending?

Yes and no. Even though our brains tell us that there's an excellent chance of everything turning out a certain way in a story, our emotions —heart, guts, sex—get us involved in the moment. We'll forget the odds, and suddenly...we don't know! The stronger the story, the more our emotions will be engaged without our brains ever knowing what happened. This is the whole field that Brian works in magnificently. Bypassing the critical mind is absolutely desirable when it comes to hearing or watching a story.

Or, as Randy likes to point out, everyone knows the *Titanic* is going to sink, but that didn't stop James Cameron's film from grossing over two billion dollars worldwide.

Why can't I just tell it my way?

I hate to tell you this, but most people overestimate their ability to tell a good story, and that probably means you, too, at least part of the time. It's like Carrie Fisher's line in *When Harry Met Sally*, "Everybody thinks they have good taste and a sense of humor, but they couldn't possibly all have good taste."

The single, easiest way to learn how to tell a good story is just to give this way a shot. It's a pattern that's worked in so many different ways that you might as well try it out.

If it's really bothering you to do it this way, if it feels like you're forcing your story, try this: Tell a different story. Set your story aside. It's okay. It'll still be there when you get back. Make up a different story. One you don't have any attachment to. Pick something ridiculous or banal, and just try telling that story using this structure. Get the feeling of doing it into your system. See how easy it is to start filing in the blanks. Who is the hero? What happens to them? What do they want? Have fun. There are no wrong choices. When you go back to your "real" story, it just might seem more flexible.

Do I have to write it just like the Logline Maker?

Well, yes. At least at first. This is traditional story structure. There's no use fighting it, and—really—no need.

For those of you who cook, you probably know that when trying a new recipe, it's best to do it exactly the way it's written, at least the first time.

Try it this way first, please, and I promise, the first time you tell your polished story to a group of people and you feel a swell of energy as every single person gets it at exactly the same time, it'll all be worth it.

Hey! Some of your Loglines aren't exactly like the Logline Maker.

Good catch. I think it's important to see that doing the Log-line Maker exactly as written works, and that once the story has gotten highly refined, making the language a little freer can work, too. Ultimately, you're going to write this in your own words, so seeing a few examples of that is a good way to think about it.

WRITING IS REWRITING

After you work with the Logline for a while, you'll have something that reads like a real story. The first real draft is a huge accomplishment. But we have a saying here in Hollywood: "Writing is Rewriting." Once you have your first version down, it's time to start making it work even better. Don't get frustrated. You'll find your way through to the best story you can make. It just takes time, effort, and focus.

If you're banging your head against a wall, frustrated with your story, scrub the kitchen floor, go for a walk, read something else, make a meal. The process of creating has natural phases to it. Ups and downs. Ebbs and flows.

Once you're locked onto a story, putting it aside for a minute or a day doesn't mean that you're not still working on it. It'll just move to a part of your mind that might be more free, less linear. Then when you go back to the writing, you'll have a clearer head and a broader perspective on how your story is working and what to do to make it even better.

And you might even get your kitchen floor really clean in the meantime.

IT'S OUT THERE

The last thing I want to share is that this elegant, innate story structure really does exist everywhere, and I want to encourage you to look for it. It's in the media all around you. In the unguarded conversations of people on the street. In the painful limp of the waiter who serves you. It's in the pile of junk that someone dumps out of their backpack to find one tiny but important thing. What people buy in the express lanes of grocery stores tells fascinating stories.

The more you turn on your critical thinking when it comes to storytelling, the more you'll be able to see these elements in the world. You'll overhear people talking about something that you recognize is a "lesson learned." You'll talk to a friend and realize that they just experienced a "catalytic event" and will now have to "take stock." You meet someone who just "achieved their goal" and they're beaming with joy. You'll know a terrific hero when you see one, and you'll see the signs of the Hero's Journey everywhere you go.

The next time you're sitting on the subway, pick a person sitting near you. Make up a story about them, starting with their ordinary world. When you're eating at a restaurant and you catch a snippet of conversation, let that be the catalytic event of a new story you're working on just for practice. When you're watching the news, notice who the hero is, what their goals are, who their allies are, and what their flaw seems to be.

Soon, you'll become an expert. And next time you sit down to write your own story, you'll be aware of the heroic journey that you, yourself are on.

Everything is a potential story. It's just out there waiting to be grasped.

BRIAN PALERMO

A familiar face to some, Brian Palermo is an actor with a wide range of performances in television, film, and top comedy venues. Palermo graduated from the University of New Orleans with a Bachelor of Arts degree in Communications. He has been a performer, director, and teacher with The Groundlings, Los Angeles' premiere comedy theatre for over 15 years. On the other side of the camera, Palermo was a staff writer on the animated series *Histeria!* for Warner Bros. and has written scripts for Disney's *The Weekenders* and *Dave the Barbarian*. He's also written and produced promotional commercials for Fox and The Disney Channel, among others.

3. IMPROV:
MAKE IT RELATABLE

WELCOME!

Hi readers! Welcome to my section of the book. It's very warm and friendly here. Grab a coffee or a rum drink and dive on in.

Okay, you've learned a lot through Randy's and Dorie's sections. I call that Overview and Story Structure Specifics. Now you've come to what many of you will find the most challenging bit—making your stories alive and relatable to your live audience. And the way I'm going to help you with this is through improvisation. Specifically, improvisational theatre games. You may think that sort of nonsense is just for actors, but it's very much for you—and anyone who wants to communicate more powerfully, effectively, and with the greatest possible reach. At the core of effective broad communication is storytelling. Improv techniques make for better storytellers, which results in better communication.

Before I throw you off the improv cliff, let me tell you how I found my way into this eccentric little corner of the world of entertainment and communications.

While I was in college at the University of New Orleans getting my Communications degree, I discovered how much fun theatre was. I was a big fan of TV and movies but had zero acting experience. The classes were challenging but in a playful way, not in a Vector Calculus way. And the fact that my odds of getting a date with cute, outgoing girls went up dramatically merely by dint of my being heterosexual was a very attractive bonus. Needless to say, I soon found myself taking a lot of acting classes as electives.

It was in one of these acting classes that I was introduced to my first improvisational theatre game. It was some sort of "mother/son" scene where we were required to improvise dialogue. I don't remember what we said, but I do remember getting laughs, feeling the rush of success and the immediate, overwhelming need to do it again.

So with a lack of preparation that has been a hallmark of my life, I auditioned for an improv group in New Orleans called "Theatre Schmeatre"—I'm not joking. (*A quick Google search reveals there is a theater company currently in Seattle with the same name. This is not related.)

This group was composed of a few students from Tulane and Loyola who were already doing shows at "Cafe Brasil," a small bar in the French Quarter. After two "rehearsals" where they taught me the improv games they did in their show, I was up on the stage in front of a handful of semi-drunk audience members.

As Dorie pointed out, a story needs a catalyst to get the action moving. To begin an improvised scene, which is basically a made up mini-story, the players often ask for a suggestion from the audience. Whatever this suggestion is serves as a catalyst to begin the scene. This establishes that the scene is indeed improvised because the performers could not have planned anything beforehand based on a random suggestion. Some common requests for suggestions are "What is the relationship between these performers?" "Where are they?" "What is a line of dialogue they can start the scene with?" etc. The idea is you take the first thing you hear and launch into the scene with improvised dialogue that justifies the suggestion.

So for the very first scene I ever improvised as a "professional," I stood on the stage ready for anything. My scene partner, who was experienced because he had done a few shows already, asked the crowd for a suggestion of "a location that this scene could take place in." Over the few half-hearted murmured offerings rung out a very loud, very clear "Dildo!" Thus, our scene was supposed to begin.

Now, I was a little shocked at first, but I've come to be very amused by this answer. Besides the enthusiasm, brevity, and immediate approval of the other patrons in the house to recommend it, I've always admired the lyrical beauty of it being a non-sequitur. I mean, it made no sense whatsoever! How can a sex toy be a "location"? I thought my partner would surely skip that suggestion in favor of another, but no. He just said, "Thank you, we take you now to a dildo."

Then he and I improvised a nursery rhyme riff about a couple of college students who lived in a dildo next to the old lady who lived in a shoe.

The scene was what I call a "beautiful disaster." It was not very clever, but it was funny. And the audience loved it. They loved our struggle to make it sensible. They loved our playfulness, our befuddlement, our mock anger, and our determination to just do it. They related to every emotion we had. And they listened to every word we said.

That's when I learned an extremely powerful communications maxim:

When they're laughing, they're listening. And that's when you deliver the message.

Improv isn't entirely about laughing, but it is about getting people to listen to you. I'll tell you how to make that happen.

Self-Aware Disclaimer:

While researching material for this book, I interviewed about a dozen friends in the entertainment industry who come from the improv tradition. I will gratefully include their comments throughout. I also have anecdotes to share about my own experiences in this world. And these will sometimes include name-dropping. Please read these through my intended filter, which is, "Hey! Here's a neat occurrence that serves as an example of what I'm describing, and it has the bonus novelty of including a well-known person!" As opposed to reading it as an arrogant, "I'm awesome and have shared the stage with truly notable people. So elevate your impression of me and love me more because of this association. Also, I'm awesome."

Case in point: World-renowned physicist Stephen Hawking once saw me perform at The Groundlings theatre in Los Angeles, and I was lucky enough to meet him afterward. Through an aide reading his computer screen over his shoulder, Hawking told me that I was "great" in the show. He was referring specifically to an improvised bit I did in the show where I mock analyzed the handwriting of random members of the audience. Pushed to find a reason for sharing this, I'd say that I bear eyewitness testimony to the fact that one of the smartest men in history said that I was "great" at improv. That should establish my bona fides a lot more than you Googling me will do.

Bonus for me: this totally one-ups Randy's Hawking story!

Now, you're probably reading this book because you want to improve your communication skills, so your message will have maximum reach and effectiveness. The best way for you to do that is to use tools that will reach the broadest segment of listeners/readers/viewers.

I'm the guy who's going to lead you to the broad side of communication. I'll help you to re-set the way you deliver information so it has a better chance of getting through to a broader audience. I'll try to get you to come down out of your head (cerebral) and into your heart and gut (emotional). Because you'll reach more people that way. As Randy pointed out in his section (and does a terrific job explaining in more detail in his first book), the more you come down out of your head, the bigger the audience you will reach. I'll teach you to communicate better by using improv.

Randy and Dorie told you about the ABT and how that mirrors Hegel's dialectic triad of thesis, antithesis, and synthesis. (Though Wikipedia says Hegel barely used the term and that he credited it to Immanuel Kant.) I don't care where it comes from, it's a powerful device. Now, I'm going to be bluntly honest. I've never written a book before. I'm not going to delicately reveal my thesis in a clever metaphor or simile or some other figure of speech that I can barely identify. I'm gonna tell you what it is as clearly as possible.

Brian's Thesis: This improv stuff is not just for actors, it's for anyone who wants their message heard. It's for YOU.

PART ONE

SO WHAT THE HELL IS "IMPROVISATION" EXACTLY

Improvisation (n): to compose and perform or deliver without previous preparation; on the spur of the moment; extemporaneously; from whatever is available.

I realize that this is probably the very opposite of what you think communicating vital information is all about. When most people think about communicating important messages, they feel it must be prepared, reliably fact-checked, and based on specific, relevant evidence. A lawyer doesn't usually head into a trial planning to "wing it." A politician would probably never give a major speech without a script.

It is very important that I point out that—though it has been made more accessible as a medium for comedy—improv is not just about humor. Laughter is important; we'll discuss that in further detail later, also. But do not get tied up in the false concept that improv is merely for creating comedy. It's for creating—period.

Very often, improv IS funny. But we are not trying to teach you to be funny. We want you to use improv techniques to help you create the skills to connect more powerfully with your audience while telling your story.

Improvisation techniques can help you **make** your story by fostering creativity. And, more importantly, improv can help you **deliver your story more effectively**. Trying to be funny doesn't come into it at all.

In our context, we'll speak of improv as mostly theatre games. And henceforth I'll just call it "Improv." (You'll adapt. I have great faith in your ability to do so.) It can be scary. One of humans' greatest fears is public speaking. Improv and theatre games can be even more intimidating as they are basically public speaking—without a script. I know that this idea is very much outside the comfort zone of most people. Think of improv as like riding a bike or surfing. You may feel unbalanced and at constant risk of falling. And you will fall. And through falling you will learn about balance, speed, trajectory, gravity—and fun. And in our case, you'll hopefully learn how to better connect with your audience without a script and while highlighting the emotions in your delivery.

WHERE TO BEGIN?

Eddie Izzard is a British comedian and actor who is well known worldwide. I've had the great fortune to perform with him many times in Los Angeles. He basically improvises his stand-up shows around stories and ideas that he wants to share. He started out as a street performer, interacting with hundreds of people a day. He's got a ton of improv experience. So I asked him what the most effective bits of improv were for him. Here's what he told me:

"The basic rules of improvisation are rules you can use in life. The rule of 'Yes, And…' is a great positive life rule.

To take an idea and to build upon it, as opposed to blocking the idea and closing it down."
— Eddie Izzard, actor/comedian

"Yes, And..." is the most basic fundamental of improvisation. It is very powerful and is a fitting place to start your introduction to the techniques.

"YES, AND..."

This refers to the dual responsibility of every improviser to agree with whatever has been established by others before him in a scene (saying "Yes") and to add more information to the scene ("And..."). The ellipsis implies more info to follow.

It is an incredibly important tenet of improv. It focuses you on being open minded and being willing to build the scene, two necessary ingredients of Creativity.

Here's a quick example in dialogue form. Picture this scene between two fictional improvisers named Stacy and Jason. The first improviser might say:

Stacy: "Good morning, Dad. You look happy."

And the second improviser might add:

Jason: "I am. I just quit my job!"

Now, Jason may have had a different idea in mind for the scene or, better yet, absolutely no idea for the scene. But by applying the "Yes, And..." technique, he has to accept everything Stacy has said ("I am.") and add more information ("I just quit my job.")

Just that simple. Now let's look at the same opening line without a Yes.

Stacy: "Good morning, Dad. You look happy."

Jason: "I'm not your father."

This will generate a laugh from the jarring nature of the incongruity, but this refusal (lack of agreement) either ends the scene or begins a series of questions in the audiences' mind that takes them out of any possible story you might create. Is the daughter crazy? Is the father? If he's not her father, who is he really? Who is the daughter really? Does he really look happy? Is one of them lying? Are they both lying? And the questions are almost endless. And while the audience is asking themselves all of these questions, they are not really hearing anything else you are trying to communicate. The connection is lost.

The lack of "Yes" just creates problems and prevents connection with both your scene partners and the audience. So you see the power of agreement. It is the essence of teamwork. And the open-mindedness required by immediate agreement allows for real creativity and spontaneity to flow. Improvisers know this: Be Open To New Information.

The second aspect of this fundamental technique, the "And..." can be any bit of new information, as long as it's relevant to the first line. Thus, the scene can proceed in almost any direction.

After the opening two lines:

> Stacy: "Good morning, Dad. You look happy."
> Jason: "I am. I just quit my job!"

The game continues:

Stacy might continue by saying,

> "That's terrific! Now you can take that trip around the world!"

or "Oh, my god. Without your job we could lose the house!"
or "You deserve time for yourself, since Mom left."
or "Aw, Dad, now I'm going to have to get a job."
or "Dad! If you quit, that means you're embezzling again!"

You get the point. It's limitless. The player who speaks next adds whatever information they wish. And the next player agrees to whatever that new info is and adds another bit of info. This pattern continues, and that is how an improv scene is built. And any of the above scenarios of daughter / father conversation could easily happen in real life. It's relatable. It's Connection with the audience.

To illustrate the importance of "Yes, And..." let's try the same experiment with a "Yes, But..."

Stacy: "Good morning, Dad. You look happy."
Jason: "Yes, but I'm really depressed."

Completely different scene. The "And..." forces the respond-ing improviser to build upon what the first improviser has begun. "Yes, But..." changes the entire game so that the sec-ond improviser is in control of the story line. It's akin to the second improviser saying, "Yes, I heard your line, But I like my idea better so I'm gonna say this." Or "Yes, I heard you make sounds, But I wasn't really listening because I was thinking of what I was going to say, which is not related to your nonsense, but it's something I'm more comfortable with and I think it will get a laugh and here it is."

It's ungainly in its transcribed form and even more so when performed this way.

**It is important to clarify a point here. Randy writes and speaks of our "And, But and Therefore" form where the conjunction "But" is used to shake the storyteller out of merely listing information and provide a catalyst to move the story forward. It's very useful in progressing the narrative, because writing is a completely different medium from performing. Using "But" during improv exercises and games negates the teamwork that allows creativity to flow. So while you do want to use "But" when writing and telling your story, you don't want to use it while improvising.

Annnnnnnnd just for fun, let's try the same experiment with a "Yes, And…" but without relevant information.

> Stacy: "Good morning, Dad. You look happy."
> Jason: "Yup. Wombats have pouches."

While Jason did say, "Yes" and the wombat pouch information he added is new, its irrelevance derails the scene. Connection lost.

You could scramble with your partner to salvage something out of this, but then you are spinning damage control instead of clearly stating information. It's a much weaker place to come from.

One of the biggest stumbling blocks for people new to improv is "not wanting to say the wrong thing." Self-censorship is the default setting of most adults because they don't want to be embarrassed or look stupid in front of others. It's understandable.

But there is no "wrong" in improv. Nothing is written down or planned beforehand, so how can it be wrong? Anything you say is workable.

Choosing to apply this rule of "Yes, And…" allows people to engage in ideas without worrying about the consequences of right or wrong. Because there is no "wrong" in improv, you don't shut down any ideas. You just let the creativity flow across your neural connections and come out your mouth. And when your head is not worried about what you say, your heart and gut can put energy into HOW you say it. This is where the relatable emotion and connection comes in!

To touch on a point that sometimes comes up: there can certainly be offensive or off-putting or unlikable pieces of information. But even those are not "wrong."

Imagine an improviser beginning a scene by saying that he killed the world's cutest puppy. Ouch, ugh, and ick. You're gonna lose the audience because cute pupicide is not relatable. But it's not "wrong."

The next improviser could add: "Thank You! That was a rabid zombie puppy and you just saved all of the orphans' lives!"

Saying "Yes" allows something to happen. That rule is the entire reason that I'm writing this book. In my life, I've thought very little of writing a book and certainly none at all about writing a non-fiction text on communication. But when Randy asked me to be involved, I said "Yes." And…here we are.

Imagine the U.S. space program if John Kennedy asked America to work on the challenge and they said, "No." Imagine the epic story of *The Odyssey* if Odysseus had turned down the call to fight in *The Iliad*. Likewise, Luke Skywalker in *Star Wars*. Or Bilbo in *The Hobbit*. What if Dorothy woke up in Munchkin Land, and instead of questing off to see the wizard, she just stayed there and opened a fro-yo stand? Nothing would have happened. There is no connection without embracing the "Yes." You have to take that first step.

"Yes, And…" also provides a paradigm that most people recognize and are comfortable with: a pleasant conversation (as opposed to an unpleasant one or an argument). A pleasant conversation can generally be described as two or more people taking turns listening and adding to a subject by using spoken dialogue. It's universal. It's emotionally positive. It's relatable. And thus, it connects people.

Keith Johnstone, author of the seminal improv work *Impro: Improvisation and the Theatre,* offers a brilliant quote on the subject:

"There are people who prefer to say 'Yes,' and there are people who prefer to say 'No.' Those who say 'Yes' are rewarded by the adventures they have, and those who say 'No' are rewarded by the safety they attain."

Will you attain your message objectives by playing it safe?

GREG THE GARDENER:

I assert that improv is for everyone who wants to communicate their story better. So let's look broadly at communication.

To see how valuable communicating your story is, let's look at an example where there was a lack of storytelling.

There was this dude named Greg. He had a day job but his hobby was gardening. He was passionate about it. He planted and harvested and experimented with hybrids and stuff for years and kept really good records of all the stuff he learned. But then he died. Therefore, everything he learned just lay around in his room. Then, years later, some other folks found his work and published it. This allowed the world to start studying the new scientific field of genetics. And many, many things changed.

The gardener was Gregor Mendel. He died in obscurity, his work hidden away in journals no one ever read until decades later when he was "rediscovered," leading eventually to the entire subject of Mendelian genetics, which is today the foundation of all modern genetics. It's not far-fetched to suggest that humanity could be decades further along in gene research and therapies if Greg had communicated his story better. How's that for stakes? My point is that even if you have the most groundbreaking information in the history of humankind, if you don't communicate that information effectively, your work is moot.

Communicating is important. And it is a learned skill set. This book is about connecting with your audience through storytelling. Connecting is communicating effectively.

We'll start very broadly. "Communication" sounds easy. Many people believe that just talking in front of other humans is "communicating." (See Figure 11.)

Figure 11: A False Equivalency

Many believe that communication equals one person talking and another hearing. That's barely close to what's needed for good communication.

But of course that is an anemic simplification. The only sure things in that equation are that someone is talking and some auditory signals are being picked up by another brain. Unless the others who hear the message actually listen and **comprehend** it, there has been no communication. Just politely patterned noise.

In its most basic definition, Communication is the sharing of information from a Transmitter to a Receiver.

And **both participants** have a responsibility to perform their side of the equation to the best of their ability for there to be genuine communication of ideas from one to the other. That means what I call "active listening." I define this as listening while actually focusing on the speaker and trying to understand what they mean. It is not just waiting for them to stop speaking so you can start again. You must have your brain centered on the speaker and not be thinking of what you're going to say next. It means setting aside your agenda while concentrating on your partner. These are improv staples.

And anyone communicating complicated messages to a group of those who are not their peers is at a particularly large disadvantage. How many of you have given a presentation and thought it went well but were befuddled by the lack of response from the audience? That's rhetorical. You don't have to actually answer. I can't hear you anyway.

Why did it go awry? The first stumbling block in this situation is that the audience questions why they should listen to you. You may be presented as an expert, and you may be a very good Transmitter. But that's not good enough. If they are not actively listening (receiving and comprehending), you ain't gonna be communicating much.

How do you encourage your audience to be good Receivers? You encourage them to listen more by being someone they want to listen to.

This part is simple; human beings will listen to others that they relate to. And here we have my central message. I have a lot to tell you, but if I had to pick just one thing (a lot like Randy's pointing toward the "one word" of your message) this would be the word—"Relatable." That may not be a word that you think of often, but by the end of what I have to say, you'll never forget it. The more people can relate to you, the easier it is to get them to hear everything you say.

I'M LIKE THEM! I'M REALLY LIKE THEM!

> "You know what I feel towards this android?"
> "Empathy?"
> "Something like that. Identification. There goes I."
> — Philip K. Dick, *Do Androids Dream of Electric Sheep?*

In his futuristic science fiction story, Philip K. Dick's protagonist, Rick Deckard, feels empathy for an android. This is problematic as he is tasked with "retiring," or killing, that android. One of Dick's themes in this story is the continuity and even growth of human emotions in the face of staggering advances in nonhuman technology. I believe this resonates with so many fans of his work because nearly all human beings innately have this ability to feel empathy toward other human beings. It's relatable.

Merriam-Webster Dictionary defines "Relate" as: "(v) - to bring into or establish association, connection or relation." If you want to connect with your audience, get their attention, convey information and possibly move them to act, you must be relatable.

It's simple biology: People are animals. Animals are instinctually self-preserving. Animals learn the best self-preservation techniques by studying successful examples of others of their same species and copying those behaviors. (This is why dolphins tend to school with other dolphins and don't generally hang out with oysters. At least not socially.) Animals respond to other animals that they relate to.

That's an extremely glib explanation of the science of relatability (to coin a very awkward phrase). Daniel H. Pink puts it much more elegantly in his book *To Sell Is Human: The Surprising Truth About Moving Others*: "Our brains evolved at a time when most of the people around us were those we were related to and therefore, could trust."

Human beings will naturally listen to those they relate to because they feel confident that both parties share similar experiences. If I feel we are walking the same path, I will listen to you because you may be able to help me with similar obstacles when I encounter them. That is self-preservation. It is a universal, natural instinct. And it is why people still listen more to those they relate to.

This is the most important quality lacking in most communications today: a relatable voice. Randy calls it "trustworthy and likable." I call it "Relatable." And if you lack the ability to be seen as human, you are not relatable. And it's a common challenge many communicators of difficult subjects face. The entirety of your audience is human. This should be the first filter you use when trying to communicate broadly and effectively: "Am I being perceived as relatable?"

Conversely, audiences avoid or ignore anyone unlike themselves because they instinctually feel they will have nothing important to learn from those they cannot relate to. Would a group of middle-aged coal miners in West Virginia likely listen to a teenaged surfer girl from Orange County? That's a fictional example, but let me offer one that's very real.

We (the authors) do a lot of work with people in the sciences. This includes scientists who are—still—mystified as to why the broad public doesn't share their fascination with molecular paleobotany, or whatever splendid esoteric obscurity they're always on about. That's because the broad public doesn't EVER think about your cerebral nonsense. So you talking about it— in any way—makes you unrelatable. And, Boom! You've lost your audience.

Most people don't relate to science types because most people don't live in a cerebral world of peer-reviewed minutia. The challenges are the same for economists, politicians, and bee-keepers. "Regular" people don't relate to them. "Regular" people DO relate to breakfast cereal and professional sports and Honey Boo Boo. So when you start spouting off about your splendid esoteric obscurity, you automatically lose the vast majority of the audience.

Brian's Note: Henceforth, I will lovingly use the phrase "splendid esoteric obscurity" to connote any subject that you are passionate about and have probably dedicated literal years of your life to. Basically, whatever subject you feel is not being communicated well enough that it drove you to read this book is your "splendid esoteric obscurity." That could be invasive species (critter obscurity), evolving computer viruses (technological obscurity), or the rise of China's middle class and its subsequent exponential contribution to deforestation (foreign tree obscurity).

It doesn't take much at all for an audience to find you unrelatable. Here's an example of how being cerebral can quickly lead to a disconnect.

When I read Randy's first book, with its section on "the two axes" of communication, my brain pictured "two big hatchets." He lost me. A long time ago he was a scientist and terms such as "axis" and "axes" are common jargon for him. However, they ain't for me. Prior to our work together, I rarely ever thought of even one axis, much less two. So until I turned the page and saw the chart, I didn't get what he was writing about. You can make the argument that using the word "axes" is hardly cerebral and that my vocabulary is just poor. I might even agree. But I'd also point out that—for good or ill—the vast majority of Americans, if not the world, would be in my position. Meaning, you'd have lost the vast majority of your audience. So you can fume, rail, or whine at the sorry state of terminology comprehension in the world, but if you don't attempt to communicate better from your side of the equation, you will never move an audience. Effective communication requires effort from both sides.

And if my misunderstanding of "axes" made you smile, you'd have loved my misunderstanding of "standard deviation." Apparently, in scientific research, a lot of data is quoted with a rate of standard deviation to give you an idea of its accuracy.

When Hollywood people speak of standard deviation it generally pertains to a drug-fueled, lesser sexual kink.

It is also worth noting that we "regular" folk are rarely exposed to, nor do we use, the acronyms and technical jargon that are often included in communications from larger institutions. It is not that we don't understand them; it is that we've never heard them or don't use them in our daily lives. So while you may be frustrated at having to differentiate an NGO from the AGU, it is important to do so if you want to keep connected with your audience.

As we've established, I ain't a scientist. I'm a regular guy. And so is your audience. So listen to me, and I'll help you get through to them!

HUMANIZE IT UP!

Please note that I am not in any way suggesting you "dumb down" your communications. But if you want to reach a wider audience, I am suggesting that you "human it up." Humanize your story. Make it more relatable. One word at a time if you have to. It will yield results.

Approximately 98% of the world's climate scientists are certain climate change is anthropogenic, but only 50% of the public agrees. The public doesn't listen to climate scientists because the public doesn't perceive scientists as people. They see them as weird robots with incredibly specialized information that may or may not RELATE TO THEM. So it is very easy for the broad public to ignore climate scientists.

NOW! How can improvisation make you more relatable? Improvisation helps you access your emotions, which proves to any audience that you are indeed a human being and thus a thing worth listening to because you are like them! Some people may think that they simply are not relatable enough to be a good communicator. I'm telling you being relatable is a choice. Improv helps teach you how to be more relatable.

We've found that having people participate in some very basic improvisational theatre games makes them both playful and reserved, insecure and confident, anxious and comfortable—basically it takes them all over the map of emotions. In other words, improv makes them HUMAN!

In Philip K. Dick's *Do Androids Dream of Electric Sheep?*, the presence or lack of emotion actually defines humanity. This is a wonderful bit of fiction, and very meaningful. As technologically advanced as those imaginary androids are, it is not their artificial intelligence that makes them most like humans; it is their emotion. Intelligence and cerebral logic simply will not reach as many people as emotions will.

If you wish to more powerfully connect with your audience, you must use those parts of your personality that the majority of humanity will relate to. That would be your emotions.

MORE THAN A FEELING

"Man is many things, but rational is not one of them."
— Oscar Wilde, *The Picture of Dorian Gray*

Much has been made in recent years about the fact that human beings are simply more emotional than rational. Dan Goleman's book *Emotional Intelligence: Why It Can Matter More Than IQ,* Daniel Kahneman's book *Thinking Fast and Slow*, and Malcolm Gladwell's *Blink: The Power of Thinking Without Thinking* have all repeatedly made this point. Theatre recognizes this truth and has used emotion as a device to present ideas for millennia. Improvisers are already on board with this dynamic.

To illustrate how this can benefit you, let me take you through this quick thought experiment. Suppose you are speaking to 100 random people about a subject you feel a deep affinity for. Let's say that's break-dancing jellyfish. For the purpose of the exercise, you may substitute any subject matter there. Instead of "jellyfish" you might be speaking about "the dangers of shark finning" or "school board procedure" or "bicycle brake maintenance." Whatever makes this personal for you.

Of your 100-person audience, how many do you think share the same knowledge and level of passion that you do about your precious subject? Two percent? Maybe three?

How many do you think share at least some vague curiosity about your subject? Ten or twelve percent?

Now how many of them have emotions?

That's right. One-hundred-f**king-percent! (Plus or minus a few sociopaths and ancient stoic philosophers. That's the standard deviation of this thought experiment.)

So which do you think would be the most effective tactic in getting your message across:

A. showing lots of stats and logical figures and rational graphs about break-dancing jellyfish, which few people care about?

or

B. appealing to your audience's emotions, which every person has, to get them listening and telling a story about the B.D.J?

I'm no mathematician, but I think potentially reaching 100 people is better than potentially reaching 10. Better by a factor of, like, forty-purple! You will reach a LOT more people by using emotion than you ever will with a recitation of facts.

Author Drew Westen tackles this exact paradigm as it pertains to voters' decision making in his excellent book *The Political Brain*. He has a lot of science to back up my assertion, which is, "Reach the people you want by appealing to their emotions, not their reason."

This is why not so long ago, enough Americans voted for the guy "they'd rather have a beer with" to elect him President.

They related more to him than the cerebral guy. It's that simple. And that is why being relatable is so incredibly important. Important, and hardly new. Philosopher David Hume stated as much in the 18th century when he said, "Reason is the slave of the passions." Let's put it so my regular folks will relate: "Smarts lose to Feelings."

You will never move people with your critically thought-out, peer-reviewed, evidence-based common sense unless you first appeal to their emotions.

Here's another personal anecdote that exemplifies how important emotions are compared to smarts.

While writing this book, the hard drive on my computer started failing. I spent two days at the Apple store replacing it, reinstalling the operating system, reloading all of my saved data, getting updates to all software, etc. In that time, I interviewed the "Genius" tech helper who was assisting me. He told me that the Mac Geniuses spend three weeks to get certified with such a designation. Only three days of which were spent learning the technical side of things and the rest of the time was spent learning how best to interact with the public. As you can imagine, and as I can attest to, consumers with tech problems can be very emotional. They experience frustration, fear, anger, and maybe even panic at the thought of losing 15,000 friggin' words written for a book on improv in communication! Just theorizing, mind you. I didn't actually panic. Much.

Anyway, Apple is considered one of the most innovative and profitable businesses in American history. And of course there are many variables that contribute to that success. Do you think the company's focus on their customers' emotional reaction to their products—be it awe at the newest gadget or panic at tech trouble time—is a major factor? I'm telling you it is.

Apple is a touchstone of technical (cerebral) achievement. Yet I'd argue that an equal driver of their success is their understanding of customers' emotions. And your own storytelling can mirror their incredibly successful model—substance delivered emotionally.

Along with listening more acutely and being more alive in the moment, improvisational theatre games train you to use emotion. This is what Randy calls the Vertical Axis. Taking information out of the cerebral and bringing it down into the heart and gut, making your info more emotional and thus more relatable. Improvisational theatre games humanize you and allow you to tell your story more effectively.

Here's another example of emotions enabling better communication. Think of emoticons. You know, those little representations of facial expressions formed by various combinations of keyboard characters used in electronic communications. Like this one for a winking happy face: ;-)

They're fairly ubiquitous, especially among the young crowds. And why do you think these things exist?

They are used to convey the writer's feelings or intended tone. In other words, to add emotion to the communication. This is because communicating clearly is difficult and using emotions helps the transmitter connect with the receiver. This is true whether the transmitter is a preteen girl texting her mother about the dreamy awesomeness of Justin Bieber or you talking about your splendid esoteric obscurity to your audience. Emotion equals connection.

The true origin of emoticons is highly speculative. I'm betting it came about when some 14-year-old boy wrote something inappropriate to some 14-year-old girl and wanted her to know he was sending it in a happy, flirty way and not a weird, creepy way. Adding emotion to your information crystallizes the clarity of intent and powerfully boosts your reach to your audience.

In 1967, Professor Albert Mehrabian (Professor Emeritus of Psychology, UCLA) reported what's become known as the "7%-38%-55% Rule" of human communication. The percentages refer to the relative importance of verbal and nonverbal messages.

According to Mehrabian, the three elements account differently for our liking of the person who puts forward a message concerning their feelings: words account for 7%, tone of voice accounts for 38%, and body language accounts for 55% of the liking. They are often abbreviated as the "3 Vs" for Verbal, Vocal & Visual.

What is important here is that an audience of receivers will determine whether they like the speaker (transmitter) based on how they say something, not on what they say. And being a likable (relatable) speaker is the best way to communicate your message.

So your tone of voice and body language is almost more important than what you say. If your audience doesn't like or relate to you, they will never hear or comprehend what you are saying. This is why emotion is so important in your storytelling. Because if people relate to you, they'll like you and will be much more open to what you are saying.

Improv teaches you to communicate with your whole body, including tone of voice. It helps you become a more relatable, and more likable, spokesperson. Carl Sagan and Neil Degrasse Tyson come to mind as people who were, and are, relatable spokespeople for what the public perceives as very difficult subjects. And neither was as effective in terms of likable reach as crocodile hunter Steve Irwin. Irwin's enthusiasm and charm helped him convey scientific, biological, and environmental information to children and adults around the world. A great example of a relatable voice.

I hear you saying, "But Brian, I'm not as adventurous or as fun as Steve Irwin, nor do I have his twinkly dimples." Maybe not. But improv will help you get closer to Steve's enthusiastic delivery than to Ben Stein's monotonous voice in *Ferris Bueller's Day Off*, where Stein's character epitomizes "boring" with his dry, emotionless, and apathetic "Anyone? Anyone?"

This is one of the reasons why that Obama commercial that Randy mentioned was so powerful and successful. The storyteller in it is a regular guy named Mike Earnest. And he could not have been any more emotionally connected with his namesake. He was sincere and convicted and believable—he WAS earnest. His story was so moving precisely because he was so emotionally relatable.

Emotional storytelling is why so many people are obsessed with the movie *Star Wars* but are indifferent about the actual stars in our galaxy.

WEAR IT ON YOUR SLEEVE

Emotionality

One of the best products of improv is learning how to tell a story emotionally. Almost every human that ever existed has had emotions. So use that knowledge. It is the one tactic that you know will connect you with others because everyone shares this association.

And it's the reason Randy brought me into this partnership in the first place. To help bring people out of their heads so they can communicate more effectively with their hearts (emotions) and guts (humor.)

When first learning improv, people concentrate on what they say, the actual dialogue that comes out of their mouths. This is normal because most people already know how to express their ideas through speech. The next step is to teach how to express yourself through emotions. This is the first real "actor-y" aspect of learning improv. Think of the old silent movies and how much story those actors were able to convey even without the occasional title cards with bits of script. Think of playing charades or of playing with an infant. A lot of these activities consist of you just making a happy face then a sad face then a grumpy face—what have you. Remember Professor

Mehrabian's 7%-38%-55% Rule: how you say something is almost more important than what you say. That is emotion.

Emotion is the big "get" here. Mad, Glad, Sad, and Horny are the big four. But there are hundreds of other emotional states, such as proud, insecure, aggressive, whimsical, concerned, cautious, haughty, loving, sympathetic, grieving, joyful, etc.

And any one of these—or any other emotion you can think of—will be more easily understood and instantly grasped by your audience than even the most superficial aspect of your splendid esoteric obscurity. Because emotion is a nonverbal communicative shorthand.

The joy on a child's face when receiving a pet puppy says a lot more than that child could say in words.

The sarcastic/disdainful eye roll of a teenager tells you everything you need to know about their opinion at that moment.

The comfortable happiness of a couple celebrating their 50th anniversary needs no words.

THE NRDC COUCH

A few years ago our Connection team did a workshop with the Natural Resources Defense Council. They have many employees and volunteers working on a wide range of environmental issues. In our workshop, we ask the participants to share the story they want to tell, and we endeavor to help them communicate it better. One of the workshoppers that day was Sarah Janssen, an MD with a PhD in Reproductive Biology and a Masters in Public Health. She is a senior scientist at NRDC and was working to update California legislation regarding toxic chemicals found in common furniture.

Sarah had reams of research and lots of facts and numbers about a specific chemical called "chlorinated tris." Much as I tried, I couldn't really stay focused on her story. To me, it was just a jumble of data and science-y gobbledygook. My brain quickly made up a story with a character named "Chlorinated

Tris," who was a super villain. And while my brain was doing that, I missed a lot of the important message that Sarah was trying to communicate.

We worked with her and the rest of the group all day, preaching the need for story structure and emotional reach. The group participated in our narrative and improv exercises. And a few months later, Sarah and her team produced a short video addressing this issue. It is titled *My Toxic Couch* and can be easily found on YouTube™.

Sarah did an amazing job of telling this potentially boring story with relatable emotions. She starts with the statement that she had reason to be "afraid of my couch" because "dangerous chemicals can escape into my living room, exposing me, my daughter, and my cat." She goes on to explain that chemical flame retardants in furniture foam had already been banned for over 35 years in kids' pajamas because it was shown to cause cancer. She ends with a call to action phrased this way, "My hope is that couches in California will no longer need to be filled with harmful chemicals."

This video is an excellent example of using emotion in your story to magnify the reach of your message. Sarah is extremely relatable as a mother—a person, not a scientist!—who is concerned for herself, her daughter, and their family pet. Boom! Trifecta of relatable to probably every mother in America. She narrates the video herself and her tone is sweet, yet reasoned. A likable and trustworthy voice. She opens with arguably the easiest grabber emotion-wise: Fear. She's "afraid" of her couch. But her voice makes it clear that this is just a sensible concern, not a ridiculous overreaction. So there is a little humor there also. She closes with another strong emotional driver: Hope. And in between she makes her case with the science. Adding emotions to her story made it relatable, which in turn made it much more compelling and understandable.

Telling your story emotionally is an incredible tool to make your communication more impactful and effective. The greatest value of improv, as it pertains to your ability to connect with an audience, is to teach you how to access and use your emotions (relatable) while modulating your cerebral side, which allows you to deliver a message (substantive).

Peter Guber is the former CEO/Chairman of Sony Pictures and current CEO/Chairman of Mandalay Entertainment. Guber's films have earned over $3 billion (that's "billion" with a "B") worldwide and 50 Academy Award nominations. I think he has a great grasp of effective reach. He wrote a piece for the *Harvard Business Review* titled *The Art of Purposeful Storytelling.* And the core of the essay can be summed up in this quote from him: "Although the mind may be part of your target, the heart is the bull's-eye."

Emotions are your target.

Okay, that's the broad basics of how improvisation will help you deliver your story most effectively, even though you're not an actor. Now let's look at the other side of my dialectic: the Antithesis.

PART TWO

If my thesis is: This improv stuff is not just for actors, it's for anyone who wants their message heard. It's for YOU. Then the antithesis is: No, improv is only for actors and funny people.

Here's some info, general and specific, that might suggest that improv is indeed for actors and funny types. It's important background. Enjoy.

A BRIEF HISTORY OF IMPROV

Once I was hired to host a marketing presentation for a DVD release of certain seasons of *Baywatch* at a convention of content distributors in Atlanta. I was to introduce the company's President, exchange a few pleasantries, and then bring out a surprise guest—Pamela Anderson. I then directed Pam and the President in an improvised scene structured around some of the tropes of that beach safeguarding series. To prep her for this, I had a few minutes to talk to Pamela prior to the show. Before pitching her my idea for the bit, I asked if she'd ever done any improv. To which she replied, "Honey, my life is improvised."

It is both hyperbolic and an understatement to say that Life is improvised. We all improvise every single day. You may have great ideas of what your day is like and plans for every second of it. But if you are in an accident on your way to your plans, you're improvising. If you're getting your daily coffee and they're out of cream, you're improvising. If your son or daughter brings home a boyfriend you disapprove of, you're improvising. This is another way that improvising is relatable. We all deal with life experiences, big and small, that we've not planned for. It is universal, human, and relatable.

Improv is a form of theater where all of what is performed is created at the very moment it is performed, with no preplanning. The dialogue, the characters, and the story are created collaboratively by the players as the improvisation unfolds.

Most commonly, improv is presented as a form of live stage comedy. It is sometimes used in film and television to creatively develop characters and dialogue. And occasionally, improvised material even makes it into the final recorded product. I'm very proud to have improvised a line that made it into the final cut of the David Fincher-directed film *The Social Network*. I'll tell you what the line was just to satisfy any curiosity, but it was in no way a big deal. It was not a funny line, just a believable one.

In the scene, the character, Mark Zuckerberg, is challenged by my Harvard computer science professor character with an extremely difficult and advanced technical problem. He answers it correctly while exiting the class in disgust due to some unrelated note passed to him by another student. While everyone is left slack-jawed by his obvious command of this most arcane knowledge, I replied with the scripted "That is correct."

Then, because it was a large lecture hall that he was exiting and the shot kept going, I stumbled out a "Does everybody see how he got there?" I just kept talking because Mr. Fincher did not call "Cut." Hopefully, the line made my performance more real. For the record, Aaron Sorkin won an Oscar™ award for Best Adapted Screenplay for this film. He really should share that with me.

The skills of improvisation are used outside of performance as well. Improv exercises are often used to train actors, writers, or anyone wanting to explore their creativity. It is used as an educational tool and as a way to develop communication skills. Some exercises are even used in psychotherapy.

The actual origin of improv as performance is not credibly recorded. It probably began when the first Australopithecus pantomimed that he had almost taken down a woolly mammoth by himself (when he was actually just foraging for berries).

Across Italy, from the 16th to 18th centuries, commedia dell'arte actors improvised their performances, based on established characters. And in the 1890s, theatrical directors such as Konstantin Stanislavski and Jacques Copeau—founders of two major streams of acting theory—both heavily used improvisation in acting training and rehearsal.

It's generally accepted that modern theatrical improvisation in the United States took form in the improvisational acting exercises developed by Viola Spolin in the 1940s, 50s, and 60s. She collected these exercises, now known as theatre games, in her book, Improvisation for the Theater.

Spolin influenced the first generation of improv at The Compass Players in Chicago, founded by her son, Paul Sills, along with David Shepherd. The Compass players included Mike Nichols and Elaine May, Shelly Berman, and others. Paul Sills also began The Second City, Chicago's premiere improv theatre, which has produced a stunning list of comedic actors. More on that later.

In 1979, British playwright and director Keith Johnstone wrote *Impro: Improvisation and the Theatre*, considered by many to be the staple of modern improv comedy. He also invented Theatresports, which is a popular format for improv comedy shows and the inspiration for the popular TV show *Whose Line Is It Anyway?* Many contemporary audiences will be familiar with improv games through that television series, which originated in England and had a very successful run in the United States with Drew Carey as its host. A new version has returned with Aisha Tyler as the host.

From the 1970s throughout the 1990s, a man named Del Close emerged as the preeminent improv guru. Close was an actor and teacher who trained a slew of the most recognizable comic actors from The Second City. He is thought of as a major influence on improvisational theatre.

There are improv theaters in every big city in the United States and many places around the world. Many college campuses have improv groups.

Improv games are fun and easy to learn. Like most things, there are levels of difficulty, but the most basic games can be learned by those as young as four or five years old. It's a great level playing field where one doesn't need to be athletic or brainy. There is no equipment necessary, and you don't even need a stage. If you have a brain and a mouth, you can improvise. And having a mouth is not strictly necessary, it's only a bonus. So improv is fairly ubiquitous these days.

If you have even the slightest curiosity about it, go take a class. They are readily available and they're fun. And don't let fear of making mistakes stop you. If you make a mistake in improv, no one gets hurt. It's not like making a mistake in woodshop.

An extremely important reminder here is that improv games and exercises are not necessarily designed to produce comedy. They are very often designed to cultivate players' awareness, to build a scene cooperatively, to commit to whatever happens in the moment without trying to control it, and for many other reasons and benefits. A common by-product of improv is comedy. And it's a gift to embrace when it occurs. But it is not the goal of improv to make you funny. For my purpose, the goal of improv is to make you more relatable.

*A Perhaps Trivial Side Note: Many years ago, long before the experience of directing at the DVD release, I acted in an episode of *Baywatch*. I got residual checks for that thing for more than 10 years, with information that it had aired in 20 or so countries, most of which were not English-speaking. A tiny testament to Randy's vertical axis, which touches on the broad reach of sex appeal. I can't imagine anyone would disagree with my estimate that *Baywatch* is the furthest thing from cerebral. But due to a few skimpy red swimsuits, those shows and the stories in them were seen by probably billions of people. I offer this as an example of the tenet that the further away from cerebral you get, the broader your message reaches.

SCHOOLS OF IMPROV

There are improv schools and theaters across the world that train people in this form, using improvisational theatre games. The two preeminent schools of improv in America are The Second City in Chicago and The Groundlings in Los Angeles. You've probably heard of one or the other, or both, of these very successful programs. Every single one of the below-mentioned performers was trained at one of these two schools.

Full disclosure: I am an alumnus of the Main Company of The Groundlings, so most of my personal experience in improv as a performer, director, and teacher comes from that theatre.

And many of the personal anecdotes I share here come directly through this connection.

Beyond these there are Improv Olympic, Theatresports, Upright Citizens Brigade, and many others that offer classes and training to thousands of interested students every year.

In addition to those celebrities named below, there are hundreds of other actors and writers (such as myself) who are not household names but have successful working careers. Each one of us that actually makes a living in the incredibly difficult, fickle, and competitive entertainment industry is another example of the power of improv in the real world.

BIG NAMES OF THE TRADITION

There is a fairly vast collection of contemporary film and television stars who got their training predominantly through improvisational theatre.

Here's a small sample list so I don't have to craft clever sentences to introduce two or three names at a time. If you're curious, you may search both schools online. They each have an alumni section.

Trained with The Groundlings:	From The Second City:
Will Ferrell	Alan Alda
Melissa McCarthy	John Belushi
Kristen Wiig	John Candy
Cheryl Hines	Bill Murray
Maya Rudolph	Dan Aykroyd
Conan O'Brien	Gilda Radner
Jimmy Fallon	Rick Moranis
Paul *Pee Wee Herman* Ruebens	Dan Castellaneta
Lisa Kudrow	Mike Myers
Phil Hartman	Bob Odenkirk
Kathy Griffin	Steve Carell
Ana Gasteyer	Amy Sedaris
Chris Parnell	Stephen Colbert
Jon Lovitz	Rachel Dratch
Wendi McLendon-Covey	Tina Fey
Jim Rash	Eric Stonestreet
Nat Faxon	Martin Short
	Ryan Stiles
	Keegan-Michael Key

Why are these predominantly improv-trained celebrities noteworthy? Consider their success as a metric of how much reach they have with audiences.

Let's focus on just two of the best-known names. In the past ten years, movies starring Will Ferrell have grossed over 1 billion dollars in the United States. Movies starring Steve Carell have also grossed over 1 billion dollars in the United States in the same time frame. These are two improv-trained actor/writers who have accounted for 2 billion dollars of movie ticket sales in the U.S. in the past decade. Assuming an average ticket price of ten bucks each, Ferrell and Carell communicated to approximately two hundred million people in America alone in that period. (*Try not to get bogged down in the data set. I've adjusted for the fact that both of these men appeared in *Anchorman*. And I'm aware that due to individuals seeing more than one of these movies, it's not approximately two hundred million unique audience members. But come on, man, take the point that these guys reached approximately TWO HUNDRED MILLION PEOPLE!)

And it's not just the goofily charming men who can perform this communications alchemy. The movie *Bridesmaids* made almost 300 million dollars in global ticket sales in less than one year. It was written by two improv actors, Kristen Wiig and Annie Mumolo, both of whom are members of The Groundlings. As are four of its six titular stars, Wiig, Maya Rudolph, Wendi McLendon-Covey, and Emmy Award winner Melissa McCarthy.

I'm not suggesting that by doing some improv training you'll gain the talent and attendant popularity of these wonderfully fun actors. Nor am I suggesting that you try to frame your story as a broad comedy, a category much of their work falls into. I am suggesting that learning from them, or at least learning similar tools that Will and Steve and Kristen have used may broaden your story's reach. And if you nabbed just ten percent of what they've garnered, you'd reach twenty million people in a decade.

Add to that the fact that the predominant audience of those movies is the coveted 18-49 year old demographic. Would that be a valuable audience for your messaging?

Enough rhetoric for now.

DOES IMPROV = COMEDY?

Here's a suitable quote that I enjoy:

"If you want to tell people the truth, make them laugh— otherwise they'll kill you."
— Oscar Wilde

This is very good advice and particularly true when delivering truths that people don't want to hear. Inconvenient ones, if you will. Much serious and important communication is hampered by the fact that the audience is uninterested in the subject. Sometimes the audience is disinclined to believe the subject. And sometimes the audience is downright hostile to the subject, and by extension, also to you, the messenger. Laughter is the sugar that helps the medicine go down.

Laughter may be the least likely response you think of, or want, when you design your communications. But laughter is a very effective delivery system for difficult communications. Laughter springs from humor, which relates to amusement, happiness, and pleasantness. All are relatable positive emotions that will help you communicate your message. We use improv to introduce many emotions into your communications. Laughter is highly connective because it is something that everyone can do almost from the time they are born. It's also a positive association, something that can only benefit your message.

"With improv, it's a combination of listening and not trying to be funny."
— Kristen Wiig, actress/writer, *Bridesmaids*

This is also true. Kristen and I have played together a lot at The Groundlings *(I use "played together" as substitute for "performed together." This is fairly standard improv parlance. I always use it because it emphasizes both the fun and the teamwork aspects of improv. A very accomplished improv buddy of mine, Dan O'Connor, calls improv "a pick-up game of theatre." That's right on. Plus, as a theater geek, I have to embrace any sports reference possible to make me more relatable to regular guys. See how that worked?).* And she really lives this advice. Earlier, I made a point about separating improv from comedy. You shouldn't try to be funny when improvising. You should strive for an authentic emotional statement or response to your scene partner. Usually the humor comes out of the audience recognizing a situation they've been in before. The laughs come from relating to the emotion of the scene or character.

I realize that the vast majority of improv is played for laughs. But the humor doesn't always come from witty dialogue. Often the audience laughs at the sheer immediacy and spontaneity of the improvisers. Add relatable emotional adjustments to the dialogue and improv can be very funny. Think of an exaggerated character tirade about the ineptitude of plumbers or something. A very common audience response is, "Oh, my god, my dad is just like that!" The phrase "Just like that" translates to "relatable." Boom: Connection.

And this humor is another very important aspect of why improv is so beneficial in connecting with people.

When people are laughing, they're listening. And that's when you deliver your message.

Science backs this up. Laughter produces endorphins, which the body craves. So when the audience is laughing, they are eager to get more body-pleasing endorphins. So they listen more actively. And this heightened listening means that they are more open to the information you're trying to get across. Endorphins also act as analgesics, so they diminish or relieve pain, which also leaves your audience more open to new information.

However, humor is a difficult topic to discuss and teach due to its complete subjectivity.

There's an old Hollywood adage that says, "Tell a joke and half of the audience will laugh; point a gun and everyone ducks." Both of these refer to the emotion of the moment. Fear and self-preservation direct everyone to react to the gun. This is why politicians often use scare tactics to garner votes. Fear motivates action. Fear is a stronger emotion than amusement and humor, which will only get half of an audience to react. If you're lucky. Professional stand-up comedians need to have a very high "batting average" of material that works for broad audiences to be successful. Let's say they have to "bat" in the 800s to have a good career. You can imagine how crazy hard that is. Comedians commit their lives to finding material that makes the majority of the audience laugh a majority of the time. It's very difficult.

Funny people recognize the value of improv to make things even funnier. I trained and played at The Groundlings with Chris Parnell, an actor and good friend of mine. He is very talented and has a wonderful career. I asked him how improv affected his work.

"I almost always expect to do some improvising if I'm working on a film, and it seems like the funnier the script is to begin with, the more the director encourages improvisation. Improv can help you find laughs and moments that, while still making sense in the context of the scene, weren't there in the script before."
— Chris Parnell, actor, *Saturday Night Live, Suburgatory*

So in our Connection Storytelling Workshops, we don't try to teach people to be funny. It's just too intangible and off-subject for a one-day workshop. With improv, however, we DO teach people to stay present in the moment and not to get caught up in a fully prepared script. This presence often yields laughter, as it allows you to react and interact with ANYthing that happens. Imagine attending a talk about, say, using ultraviolet light to improve the cleanliness of operating rooms—a current epidemiological theory. Yeah. I almost fell asleep typing that sentence. It is a dry topic to the majority of the populace. But if someone interrupts the speaker and they shoot back any sort of rejoinder—witty or not—it will break the boredom and probably cause a laugh.

We're not suggesting you try to make a standup routine out of your splendid esoteric obscurity. We are suggesting that you use humor as a spice and sprinkle it into your presentation. It has a very high efficacy rate even in—particularly in—communications that are "serious." There is a very low expectation of humor in such communications, thus there is a very high appreciation when some slips in. And, again, the audience is listening more actively. And will be more attentive to your message.

Now remind yourself of all the improv-trained comedic actors I listed above. Remember the billions of dollars in ticket sales and the reach that indicated? This is a reminder that those actors, in those movies, reached those numbers of audience members primarily through laughter. Getting laughs gets attention. And isn't that what you'd like to bring to your splendid esoteric obscurity?

Once they're laughing, they're listening. That's when you deliver your message.

PART THREE

So there was a section that seemed angled to convince you that improv is only for funny people. It was chock-full of quotes from actors famous for being funny, and they are all trained in improv. And there's sooo many of them! Plus, there was theatre history. That can only be for actors, right? Well, I hold that the previous section was just more information for adopting my argument:

Synthesis: Improv is for everyone: actors, funny people, and anyone who wants to communicate more effectively. Improv benefits everyone. Improv benefits you.

Still want more? Another proof that improv is for more than actors, consider the fact that major corporations have embraced it.

THESE GUYS PAID FOR IMPROV?
MUST BE VALUABLE

For the past forty years or more, corporate clients have tuned in to how improv workshops benefit their companies. In addition to all of the advantages we've discussed (and more below), improv helps with presentational skills, team building, and clarity of communication in the workplace. It is helpful within any organization as well as training employees to better interact with outside clients.

Here is a sample of companies that I have personally taught improv workshops to:

Walt Disney Company	Lee Jeans
Nike	Segerstrom Center for the Arts
Universal Studios	Natural Resources Defense Council
Vans (apparel)	Heal the Bay
National Park Service	ASLO (The Association for the
7 For All Mankind	Sciences of Limnology and Oceanog-
Boston Consulting Group	raphy.)
The North Face	

And a cursory glance at some other improv theatre sites shows that they have taught to these other corporate clients: (additionally, from The Groundlings, Second City, Improv Olympic, Improv Asylum and Improvolution!)

Calvin Klein	Red Bull
Baskin Robbins	Gillette
Farmers Insurance	Raytheon
Zurich Insurance	Dunkin Donuts
United Way	Staples
Chicago Sun Times	Prudential
Cern (Geneva, Switzerland)	Radio Shack
Merrill Lynch	Bank of America

These companies spend real money to gain communication insights from improv. It's a proven benefit. Some corporations seek out improvisation workshops because they've tried, and are perhaps tired of, military-style ropes courses or shoulder massage circles or playing pass-the-orange-under-your-chin games. All of which have team building and amusing results, I am sure. And I am very much on the side of fun in the workplace, as it generally begets creativity, relieves stress, and thereby increases productivity. I believe the "takeaways" of improv workshops are vital to a healthy, constructive, and productive workplace. And those takeaways are even more salient when your specific goal is to communicate your story most effectively.

THERE'S A "CENTER" FOR THIS STUFF?

Another example of improv's legitimacy when specifically applied to communicating serious issues is the Alan Alda Center for Communicating Science at Stony Brook University. SUNY Stony Brook has broken new and innovative ground by partnering with Alda, a well-known comic actor, who is also an alumnus of The Second City. The center's goal of teaching scientists improv is very similar to our goal for everyone, not to turn them into actors but to help them connect with audiences more effectively.

BENEFITS OF IMPROV FOR EVERYONE

You want to be a better speaker; learn to be a better listener. You want to convince other people; learn to connect more with other people.

You want to motivate people to act; appeal to their emotions more than their reason.

I know that these statements may sound like banal motivational generalities, but they are meaningful. If you listen and connect more, you will be better able to identify your audience's mindset and match it so your message is more readily accepted. It is not a coincidence that "motivate" and "emotion" derive from the same root. If you want to do the former, you must use the latter. Emotions are so important that I spent a huge amount of time on it in my first section.

Do Listening, Connection, and Motivation belong to only one group of people, such as actors or funny people?

No, these would benefit anyone, particularly those trying to tell their story. And these are the advantages improv will teach you.

One of the most common responses to improv performance is, "That was so clever." Many audience members feel there's a need for supernatural intelligence in order for improv to work well. This implies that improv is a brainy activity. But it's not really. Improv is visceral. It relates to feelings much more than intellect. It brings you down out of your head and helps you communicate on a more instinctive level. That is precisely why more people respond to stories told with emotion than to stories that appeal to reason—it's instinctive. The evidence for this assertion is described much more elegantly and in much greater depth in two excellent books: Drew Westen's *The Political Brain* and Malcolm Gladwell's *Blink: The Power of Thinking Without Thinking*.

Most of the public does not live in their heads, and the ones that do don't live in YOUR head. If you want the ideas in your brain to reach out and connect with others, improv is a brilliant tool. And many of the improvisers I interviewed for this book spoke to how improv benefits people in all aspects of their lives.

Jim Rash is a friend of mine from The Groundlings. He is an Oscar™ winning cowriter of The Descendants (and semi-famous for mocking Angelina Jolie's awkward leggy pose). He's also a recognizable actor from the TV show *Community*. He put this aspect of improv-for-life very well when I asked him how it had helped him professionally.

"I think the biggest revelation about improv to me, which really should have been clear from the beginning, is how many of its core principles are things that we should be doing in our day-to-day lives. Among the most important: Listening, getting out of our own heads, and being in the present. Improvisation has helped me to be a better actor and better writer. But honestly, it can help you to be a better person."
— Jim Rash

Here's a quick sampler of what improv offers:

NOW. NO, NOW! NO, RIGHT NOW!

Spontaneity

Forget being alive in the moment; that is so pre-Twitter's 140 character postings. Because of its immediacy and its refusal to plan, improv teaches you to be more alive in the split-second! And a lively Transmitter is a more effective one. Again, think Steve Irwin versus Ben Stein.

Improv teaches techniques to help you hone your awareness to take advantage of every second to better communicate your message. When performed for an audience, the improvisers on stage can react to each other instantaneously. They can even react to the audiences' reactions of laughter, groans, or silence. Improvisers can adjust their choices to follow what's working. On the fly. Immediately. Without being tethered to preplanned scripts, lighting, stage movement, props, music, or anything else, they can just go with whatever's working on stage and with the audience.

Once when I was improvising a scene with Eddie Izzard, a female fan of his in the front row kept offering her own lines of dialogue for the action on the stage. She desperately wanted to be involved. Everyone in the theatre could hear her, and it was a distraction. So in the middle of our scene, I turned to her and included her—in a way. I labeled her "Aunt Edna" and said that she'd finally arrived with her customary treats. Then I physically stepped off the stage and took her purse. I brought it back on stage where Eddie and I went through the contents, commenting on whatever we found. We wound up handing out all of her mints. (The price you sometimes pay for sitting front row.) The audience went nuts. The immediacy of the moment just shot energy through the whole house of about 200 people. It was a great moment of being alive in the second—brought to you by improv.

Now, what would have happened if, at that precise moment, I turned to the audience and said, "Ocean acidification is real and we have to act now." Well, it would have been absurdly jarring and disconnected in that context. But I guarantee that they would have heard me. Their attention was rapt. I merely offer this as an example of the power of extemporaneous speech. You want to bring a little spontaneity to your storytelling.

HYPER-UBER-META LISTENING

Awareness / Listening

Due to the nature of improv being created on the spot— from your brain's synapses to your mouth—you have to be hyperaware of what's going on around you. You must be alert to what your scene partner says and does, how they move, what you say and how you move, how the audience reacts— everything. This awareness allows you to build on what has just been established. You do not default to story lines or characters that have been created before. You do not try to cram in your great Christopher Walken impression or your joke about the clumsy optometrist. You work with whatever was created three seconds earlier. In order to do this properly, you must raise your awareness to intense levels. This is the active listening I talk about. If, when improvising a scene, you miss the fact that your scene partner called you "Mom," and you proposition them flirtatiously, you've just chucked that whole scene into an awkward, weird, harder-to-fix scenario. Or at least you've moved it geographically to Mississippi. Either way, instead of creatively building onward and upward, you're now tap-dancing sideways to justify that missed communication. Acute Awareness prevents the problem and allows you to go forward.

Improv helps train your hyper awareness by requiring all of your senses, real and imagined, to fully participate. Though taste and smell don't really come up that often, if they do, I guarantee it will be a unique experience! Most of your awareness is funneled through your senses of touch, sight, and sound. As I mentioned earlier, it's not enough to just hear what's going on, you have to listen acutely and actively. Listening skills are necessarily heightened through improv. And they are invaluable when telling your own story.

While compiling material for this book, I interviewed about a dozen friends in the entertainment industry who come from the improv tradition. I asked how improv affected their work and lives. And what, if any, improv skills helped the most with their specific storytelling. You will see from the brief sampling below; "Listening" was a big, common reply.

"Improv has definitely helped me in so many ways. I've been required to improv in many acting jobs. And it's made me a better listener in my everyday life, which helps everything."
— Stephanie Courtney, actress, *"Flo," the Progressive Insurance girl*

"At its core improv is a skill of listening, connecting, and responding authentically. When I get nervous I tell myself, 'Just listen to what they say, hear them, connect, and trust that you'll have a response.'"

— Jerry Trainor, actor, *iCarly*

"As for how it helps communication—the concept of Yes, And makes you a good listener. You aren't trying to force your ideas; you become used to seeing value in everyone's ideas. Makes you less scared of public speaking—even now when I have to MC an event or something, I don't get quite as stressed because I know I can play off of what is going on in the room in the moment."

— Rachel Dratch, actress/writer, *Saturday Night Live*

"The best improvisers are those who really listen. The more you listen, the more you know. The same rule of listening can be applied in your business life and your personal life."

—Brad Sherwood, actor, *Whose Line Is It Anyway?*

Odds are good that you yourself have seen these performers (Stephanie's ubiquitous "Flo" is probably somewhere in your periphery right now). Imagine the reach they have and that you can achieve with some improv training. I would certainly advise anyone who wants to communicate better to take an improv class. And in the meanwhile, to get your feet wet, I have provided an appendix of improv exercises that you can do on your own.

SPIFFY, UNIQUE MAKE-EM-UPS

Creativity

The "Yes, And...." technique prevents improvisers from saying "No" to anything that's offered by anyone in an improvised scene. This perpetual affirmative process allows ANY idea to be cultivated and built upon. And this leads to genuine creativity.

Quick Thought Experiment: Suppose we are partners and are tasked with creating a new vehicle that can travel in the air and under the water for short bursts of time. I suggest we take an old stand-alone phone booth and duct tape 50 pelicans to it.

What is your response?

Most people would immediately question the soundness of my brain and think "that won't work." And that is correct.

An improviser will just accept the premise and add to it. "The Peli-Booth runs on fish, so I've bought a catfish farm to raise our own 'fuel.'" That is creative.

Normally, when people hear an idea, they quickly default to why it won't work. Maybe this instant negation is to save time by not wasting it. Maybe this negation is the result of decades of failed attempts at pelagic-fowl-powered-transport. Maybe it's from fear of failure or due to one's history with one's mother. For whatever reason, most people begin with "No." And this stops the idea—any idea—from growing into anything that might possibly work. It halts that train of thought. Improv teaches you to go with any idea—even as absurd as the above example. And this yields mighty creativity...if everyone is on board with using improv as a tool. We've seen the immediately abortive power of No.

My purpose is not to turn you into some absurd Dada-ist, creating abstract and farcical communications. I just want to expose you to how improv breeds creativity, which can be useful in your storytelling. I love the story of the Centers For Disease Control posting a blog with instructions on how to survive a zombie apocalypse. That is extreme creativity used in a practical, simple way that paid off very well for the CDC.

And, as I said earlier, improv also creates in you several skills that will help you deliver your message more effectively. It creates a less cerebral, more emotional and relatable delivery.

I did a movie with Harland Williams and we became pals. He is a terrifically funny stand-up comedian/actor who often plays odd characters. You may remember him as the crazy hitchhiker from *There's Something About Mary*. I asked him about his high-octane brand of creative silliness.

"Improvisation allows one to go beyond what is written on the page or prepared in one's mind. It is that delicious creative juice that seems to take you for the ride rather than you controlling it. Once you have the courage to release the improv monster, the results are supremely gratifying, the improv seems to give you wings. It's where your creative instincts and the complete unknown intersect. When you allow them to comingle and trust in them to make you do and say things even you haven't preplanned, the results are magical."

— Harland Williams, comedian/actor

LAGNIAPPE

That heading is a French word that's pronounced "lan-yap." And it means "a little something extra given as a bonus or gift." I'm using it to mean, "Okay, I'm resting my case with the dialectic, but I've got a few extra tidbits of info to give you."

CONNECTION VS. DIRECTION

I mprov trains you to build scenes or stories together. Think of it in these terms: "I add one line of information, then you add one line. We continue that dynamic, and together we build the scene." It's a creative, theatrical see-saw and improv is the fulcrum. You are connected to your scene partner so you can create together. If only one person is controlling the course of the creation it is direction, not connection. Improv teaches (forces) you to work with others in a very connected manner.

When I teach the improv basics, either in a class for The Groundlings or at a Connection Storytelling Workshop or a corporate workshop, I can always tell the control freak/Type A Personality/Virgo contingent of the students. They are very good at driving a scene with their own ideas. They are generally very bad at working with others in this amorphous art form. In other words, they're good with direction but not with connection.

I don't want to hit the connection metaphors too hard, but it is one of the best benefits of improv training, and it is the name of the bloody book!

Think of improvising with someone else as building a bridge. You start constructing something on one side of a canyon (the unknown). And based on where you begin your side of the bridge, your partner on the other side of the canyon begins building theirs. You adjust for their materials and their architectural aesthetic and continue building towards them. They do the same. And so on until you both reach each other in the middle. Voilà—Connection.

My friend, Cheryl Hines, whom most of you know as Larry David's wife on *Curb Your Enthusiasm*, has an interesting way of using improv techniques to produce connections in her professional life.

"One very important element of improv is to assume a relationship. I use this idea every day. Before I walk into a room to audition or take a meeting, I think about what relationship I already have with the person I'm about to meet. I assume that we have a friendship, we like the same things and we're both working together to make this TV show/film great."
— Cheryl Hines, actress, *Curb Your Enthusiasm, Suburgatory*

THE POWER OF CONFIDENCE

I'm sure you're familiar with Jay Leno, the stand-up comedian who has hosted *The Tonight Show* for over 20 years. He has massive reach with audiences across America. I spoke to him specifically about how improv can help shape the crowd's view of you. Here's what he said:

"Improv is the essence of intelligence. If you appear to be talking off the top of your head, you'll come off smarter and be a more effective speaker."
— Jay Leno, stand-up comedian/host, *The Tonight Show With Jay Leno*

I think this is a really important note. If you are talking off the top of your head—in other words, not trying to remain rigidly in lockstep with a script, you are seen as more knowledgeable about your subject. This translates emotionally as confident and assured. This is another important aspect of being an effective storyteller. Improv tools help you to be more comfortable speaking with and to people.

Improv techniques enable you to become confident while making up silliness such as pelican-powered phone booths. Imagine how confident you will be with your story that you know so well and have written yourself. Self-assurance is an important quality for a storyteller, as long as it doesn't evolve into arrogance. That is less relatable.

Improv might seem scary, but jump in! You'll build confidence as you go. Focus on the connections that you will make, and you'll soon see the benefit in your communications, and daily life, as you get more comfortable with it.

"SO LONG, FAREWELL, AUF WIE-DERSEHEN, GOOD NIGHT"

> "I'm so glad we had this time together."
> "Thanks for the memories."
> "That's all, folks."

Any of those quotes ring a bell? If you're of a certain age, of course they do. And they're each hard-wired to emotions. That's why you remember them.

The first is from the freshly scrubbed Von Trapp children bidding good night to the adult party in The Sound of Music (relatable to anyone who was ever a child who didn't want to go to bed, which is to say, EVERY PERSON who has ever lived!).

The second was Carol Burnett's signature show-ender. A touching adieu after an hour of laughter. Very effective and memorable.

The third was Bob Hope's sign off. He sang it for decades, and each time it carried a little bit more weight because he had added a few more memories since the last time he'd sung it. I've gotten misty-eyed watching him do so.

The fourth was Porky Pig's message at the end of most Looney Tunes cartoons. Again, a short wave goodbye after laughter. It sticks with you.

Relatable. Emotional. Humorous. This triad will help you reach almost any audience.

Thus ends my little treatise on how to improve your communications. So I leave you with this personal message: Thank you for reading. I hope you found it helpful.

And for you readers under 40, imagine me arrogantly dropping the microphone as I bark, "I'm out, bitches!"

4. ACTION: APPLYING THE WSP MODEL

Randy Olson

MAKING THE LONG STORY SHORT

Okay, how's everybody doing—starting to develop a little bit of "story sense"? We've covered quite a bit of ground. I gave you the basics of roughing in a story; Dorie took you into the depths of the Hollywood perspective; then Brian showed you how to make your story more relatable. Now it's time to bring everything together; hopefully giving you a feel for how it works in the real world.

In this section are three fictional scenarios to show you how the WSP Model can be put to use finding and shaping stories.

The WSP is not any sort of a panacea, and because good storytelling remains half intuitive, we can't take you the whole distance for crafting a good story. But as we've said all along, we've been using this approach for the past three years in our workshops and have seen its power. Over and over again we watch as participants take their disorganized, ambling story and start to give it some shape—like turning a lump of clay into something recognizable, even if it's only an ash tray as a starting point.

Or, to put it in Churchillian terms (if we can assume he's the guy who said that thing about needing extra time for a shorter presentation), this is a simple way to make a long story short.

SCENARIO 1: EXISTING STORY: THE STORY ALREADY EXISTS; THE WSP HELPS STRENGTHEN IT.

Stephanie Wilson is a concerned mother of a sixth grader in the suburbs of Nashville, Tennessee. There are no computers in her son Jake's classrooms. Next week is the monthly school board meeting where they allow time for parents to address the school board with specific concerns. She has just read the first three chapters of our book (she got an advanced copy!) and absorbed the basic elements of the WSP Model. Now she wants to put it to use in preparing for this big opportunity to speak to the board.

She begins with the one WORD that is at the core of what she will be trying to convey. Her concern is about "computers," but that word doesn't say much. She wants something that has more of a human feel capturing the overall dynamic of her concern.

She's doesn't want to convince the board to make the school into a magnet program for computer sciences; she knows there are clear financial limits for a public school. All she's really asking is that her son gets the chance to have a learning opportunity equal to other school districts. She gets closer to her one word with "equality," but that still doesn't have the depth of what she's seeking and maybe feels too much like discrimination is involved, when it clearly isn't. Finally, she settles on "fairness." That reaches deeper inside of people—everyone just wants kids to have a fair shot in the world.

If this was all she had for a presentation, it wouldn't amount to much. It's only a start, but it is the core element. If she ends up engaging in a dialogue with the board members and loses her train of thought, she can revert back to it, saying something like, "Look, all I'm asking for is a little fairness; it just isn't fair for them to be disadvantaged when it comes to computer skills."

Now she proceeds to the one SENTENCE using the ABT template. This may seem simplistic, but you'd be amazed how many people get in the middle of arguing for something, yet when you ask them, "Can you tell us what you want, in a single sentence?" they stumble and waste precious time trying to make their message concise on the spot. There's really no excuse for that lack of preparation.

So she first considers the overall issue, using the ABT to craft a possible opening sentence along the lines of, "We have a great school here AND our students are eager to learn, BUT our computer resources are not what they should be, THEREFORE, I'm asking the Board to consider allocating more funds this year for the purchase of computers for the sixth grade class."

And there she has it. One sentence that encapsulates the issue. If she leads with that sentence there should be no looks of confusion, only anticipation of further detail. Which then opens the door for her to use the true power of storytelling to make her case in the form of the one *paragraph*.

At this point, she could just go the expositional route by presenting pieces of information she considers compelling. She could maybe cite a recent study that shows significantly higher computer skills among sixth grade classes who have a certain ratio of computers to kids than schools with a lower ratio. But think back to the Neurocinematics research.

If you just present facts, the brains of the board members will head off into various different directions. However, if you tell them a compelling story, you will draw them into greater synchrony of thinking—meaning that you can lead them more effectively in your desired direction.

So she wants to follow that opening sentence with a story, and she knows exactly what she wants it to be. She wants to tell about her close friend Tamara Jenkins, who lives in Omaha and has a daughter, Sophie, who is a senior in high school and was just accepted to all five universities she applied to. At the core of Sophie's success has been the interviews she's had at each university, where she has told about her senior project, which was a study of mortgage financing plans of six local lenders.

From an early age, Sophie has been fascinated with homes in general. When little girls her age were playing with dolls, Sophie showed little interest in how they dressed the dolls. Instead, she wanted to know, "What kind of house does your doll want to live in? Does she want a split-level ranch, a two-bedroom craftsman, or maybe an L-shaped stucco with a sloped roof?" Her poor friends would be stumped, having no greater opinions than, "My dolly just wants a house."

But it was sixth grade when things changed for Sophie. Through a Nebraska state supported program, her school managed to buy enough computers that there was one for every two sixth graders. The students were encouraged and guided in delving into their own interests using the computers. That was the year that Sophie discovered the MLS—Multiple Listing Service. She discovered it because she had access to computers.

Without the computers, Sophie would have still been interested in houses, but with the exposure to computers and with guidance she moved her interest to a whole new level.

By eighth grade she was running tutorials for the teachers in her school who were looking to buy homes, by tenth grade former teachers were tracking her down for advice, and finally for her senior project she did the mortgage financing study that won her first place in a competition sponsored by a local realtor. It's an amazing story, and it all tracks back to that sixth grade class that opened her world up with computers.

So Nancy has a good story to tell. But when parents are given the chance to speak to the School Board, there is a green light/yellow light/red light display on the podium limiting their time to exactly three minutes. That is the challenge she now faces—how to make sure this story stays within the time limit, yet be as powerful and compelling as possible. This is where the Logline Maker comes into play.

To get the overall "rough" story clear in her head, she again uses the ABT to establish the structure at the simplest level, but now she uses it to summarize the individual story rather than the overall issue.

She writes down that this is a story about a girl in Omaha who had an early interest in real estate, AND her ability to cultivate that interest over the years proved to be her most important asset in applying to college, BUT the pivotal opportunity for her took place in sixth grade when her school had the computer resources to let her really catch fire on this interest; THERE-FORE, our own school district should help our kids have the same sort of opportunity by allocating the funds to purchase computers for the sixth grade class. And once again, it's only *fair* that they should be given this opportunity.

She now reviews the Logline Maker to prepare for her call to her friend Tamara. Instead of just saying, "Tell me the whole story," and taking notes, she now has a set of targets that point her to questions like "What was your daughter's life like before the access to computers?" (the *Ordinary World*). "What caused the school to purchase computers?" (the *Catalytic Event*). "Why was it later important that she get into college?"(the *Stakes Got Raised*).

There's so much that could be asked about her daughter's story, but the Logline Maker helps her stay focused on the most powerful details. The overall result for Stephanie is that she's not just "swinging in the dark," in wanting to bring to bear the power of storytelling in making her case to the board.

Using the WSP she has a systematic way to approach her storytelling needs. It's not a guarantee for success. Remember, it's providing only the cerebral part of the equation. At some point you also have to have some instinctive feel for what is and isn't going to work. But at least it gives you a direction to head in gathering the basic elements for a powerful and persuasive story.

SCENARIO 2: SEARCHING FOR A
STORY: THE WSP AS CHECKLIST

John Petersen has a challenge on his hands. He's a civil liti-
gator in Philadelphia who has taken on the case of a young
businessman accused by his partner of embezzling $80,000
from their company. It's just another case, but John feels bad
for this guy. The client's company is a chain of computer and
electronic stores in the region that have done well, but because
this young man and his partner who founded it with him were
such good friends from college, most of their agreements were
verbal. Which means it's going to come down to one man's
word against the other in court. On Monday morning.

Friday afternoon, having prepared the paperwork as best as
possible, John goes to a bar in his client's neighborhood that he
knows he frequents. It's "afternoon empty"—nobody there but
a sports fan watching the basketball game and a young couple
at a corner table who look like they're from out of town. John
takes a seat at the bar, orders a whiskey on the rocks and asks
the bartender if he knows his client. The response is immediate as a warm glow with a friendly smile sweeps over the hefty
bartender's face.

Over the next hour the bartender tells one story after another
of the kindness of this guy, all of which are being recorded on
John's smartphone sitting on the bar beside his drink. As other
men show up, the bartender introduces them to John, telling
them what he's there for. The stories keep coming. Clearly his
client has touched a lot of people in the community.

On Saturday, John has lunch at the Italian restaurant next
door as the owner of the restaurant and several of his staff stop
by and tell more stories of the client—all of which are recorded
on the smartphone

By Sunday evening John is in his living room, taking notes on
the stories of the more than twenty acquaintances he's recorded.
It's obvious his client is a really decent man who would never

cheat his partner. There's a mountain of material to convince the jury. BUT, there's only going to be one morning session in court, and while all these testimonials are incredibly heartfelt, most of the people tended to ramble, telling endless side details. Not a one of them would make a compelling character witness.

It's all too much. John feels like he's back in college, having crammed for a big exam but finding himself the night before so overloaded with input he can no longer focus. He instinctively knows he should probably just try to present one truly compelling story to the jury, and he has a few in mind, but which one and how to get the point across in a concise and powerful way?

This is where the WSP Model comes into play and he, too, happens to have an advance copy of our book. He nails the one WORD not with "business" or "partner" or even "popular," but with a more human quality: "benevolence."

For now he skips the one SENTENCE and goes straight to the one PARAGRAPH—to the Logline Maker, using it as a sort of checklist of criteria for which is the best story. He begins thinking about the various terms—flawed protagonist, catalytic event, the stakes get raised as he looks over the stories he recorded. One of the stories finally jumps out at him.

One of the client's neighbors told the story of when a family on their block lost their house in a fire (*Catalytic Event*). The client, even though he always commented about how much he valued his privacy (Flawed Protagonist), took the family in, letting them live in his two guest bedrooms for six months. This was enough of a generous act to begin with, but then the business partner leveled the embezzlement charges (*The Stakes Get Raised*) and he never changed his behavior towards the family.

John replays the recording of the man telling the story and finds even more elements of the hero's journey in this story of his client. Then he goes back to the Logline Maker, using it to help him trim the story down for presentation in court.

On Monday morning as he prepares for the trial, he writes down an ABT version of what he will say to use as his opener. When the time comes to present this story, he will begin with, "My client owns a chain of computer stores AND is accused by his partner of embezzling, BUT I'm going to tell you the story of how this man showed great BENEVOLENCE which (THEREFORE) will make it hard for you to believe he would ever cheat a business partner." (Notice, you don't have to use "therefore" verbatim; it's just a structural placeholder for which other words like "so" or "which" could work just as well or better). The well-structured ABT sentence at the start will provide a solid introduction to his story so that the judge doesn't start to wonder, "What is this all leading to?" It will provide a brief "roadmap" before he heads off on his short and compelling story. And by emphasizing the word, "benevolence," they will know exactly what it's all about.

SCENARIO 3: CREATING A FICTIONAL STORY: USING THE WSP TO CREATE A SINGLE STORY FROM SCRATCH

Rafael San Miguel is a junior at the University of East Virginia and President of the Latino Student Union. At this month's meeting of the organization, with its roughly three hundred student members, he wants to recruit volunteers to organize activities in the local community engaging Latinos not connected with the university.

In previous meetings he's made the usual plea for recruiting local volunteers, citing facts about discrimination that they all face, but the response has been minimal. This time he needs more of a connection from his audience. To do this, he's decided to tell a story that will motivate the members.

He automatically knows what his one WORD is that he wants to convey: "solidarity." He wants to get local Latinos to realize they are subject to the same aspects of discrimination as students, and that together, they can improve conditions more effectively than separately.

He also decides the most effective way to reach his intended audience is by dramatizing what he's talking about by filming a short Public Service Announcement (PSA). He begins scripting a story that will convey the issue.

He now uses the ABT template for the one SENTENCE statement of his message. He boils it down to this: Latinos face a number of civil rights issues, AND there is a large enough local population to achieve the respect they deserve, BUT unless the various groups manage to combine their efforts they will never accomplish this; THEREFORE, the Latino Student Union needs to begin working to bring the local groups together in a unified effort.

He begins crafting the story of a single individual, Frederico, who was the victim of discrimination until he fought back. He creates a second ABT for this specific story. "Frederico worked as a delivery man in a college AND he had no connection or interest in the college, BUT when his employer began discriminating against him based on his limited English speaking skills he needed help, THEREFORE he found a group at the university and together they addressed his problems.

Now to strengthen the story he turns to the PARAGRAPH, with the story of a factory where the employers refuse to tolerate any langue difficulties with Latinos (*The Ordinary World*). Frederico is a quiet worker at the factory who keeps to himself (*Flawed Protagonist*). When he finds himself left out of a project that would have paid him overtime (*Catalytic Event*), he decides to contact students from the Latino Student Union (*Taking Stock*).

He continues to develop this story, eventually locking in all nine elements of the Logline Maker. Then Rafael calls up three of his closest friends on the student union and runs the story by them. Each one gives him their notes as he shapes and modifies the story until he's ready to take it public by going to his local bar.

He runs into a group of students who are members of the union to whom he tells the story. They get it. There's still a couple of points of confusion, but with their feedback, he trims the story and is ready to present it at the meeting, where it has a much broader meaning and is more compelling than just listing facts.

MAY THE WSP FORCE BE WITH YOU

These are three ways to make use of the WSP Model. The most important aspect of it is that the model itself helps build your story intuition. As you listen to others tell stories that drag, lose the audience, or don't add up, you will begin to find yourself using the elements of the WSP as diagnostic tools to figure out what's going wrong.

You end up asking yourself: What is the one word theme of this story they are telling? Can I put their story into the ABT template? Does it lend itself to the logline template, and if so, have they managed to develop the nine key elements?

The WSP Model is both creator and analyzer. It gives you a more objective, analytical approach to figure out, "What the hell has gone wrong with this mess of a story?" Which is a question that arises all too often—everywhere from Main Street, USA to the heart of Hollywood, California, every day of the year.

THE ABT VS. THE LOGLINE MAKER

To explore these two key templates a little more, let's take a look at their attributes side by side. We've put together a brief comparison of the two in the table below.

The "And, But, Therefore" (ABT) is relatively simple. It's easily accessible, easy to comprehend. So many times we've seen people hear the idea of this simple template, get it, and put it to use immediately, with no learning curve whatsoever. Just about every event, project, or program can be expressed as an ABT sentence. Which is amazing. As a result, it's very broad in reach.

But the down side is it can be too broad. Your ABT sentence might end up too vague to be effective or as a giant paragraph-length sentence that defeats the whole purpose. Still, it's worth pushing yourself to state your story using the template. Your story is almost certainly there—you just have to find it.

	ABT	LOGLINE
# of elements	3	9
Format	Sentence	Paragraph
Complexity	Simple	Complex
Strength	Breadth	Depth
Components	Informational	Dramatic

TABLE 1. Comparison of the "And, But, Therefore," and Logline Templates.

The Logline, in contrast, with its nine elements is much more complex. It's not as easy to explain, understand, or put to use quite as quickly as the ABT. It guides you through the entire "Hero's Journey" structure, and not every situation lends itself to it as perfectly or obviously as the broader ABT.

If you're at a cocktail party and someone starts rambling about a story they want to write up but "can't quite get a handle on it," you should try trotting out the ABT. Just ask them to see if they can tell the story in one sentence using it. It's a fun, effective and quick exercise. But you probably wouldn't want to ask the person with the cocktail in their hand to start itemizing the nine elements of the Logline. Wrong place; wrong time.

However, at the right place and right time, the Logline is much more powerful. The strength of it comes from two big sources. First, it has the power of specificity. (Remember the simple rule, "the power of storytelling rests in the specifics.")

Second, it is made up of dramatic, human, emotional elements. It is your pathway into the world of authentically human stories that have the potential to reach inside people. These stories connect on a deeper level.

Also, the ABT, by design, does not give you any information about what goes between the AND, BUT, and THEREFORE. On the other hand, the Logline tells you exactly what goes in the blanks. It guides you through who or what your story is about, what happens, and why, giving the story its meaning.

For example, one of the most interesting elements is "Taking Stock." A scientist recently told me a story he wanted to use in a presentation. It was about seeing a set of data on ice melting in Greenland that he felt should be released as a major statement on global warming. In his version of the story, he said he pulled a few of his fellow scientists together and they decided to take a chance by putting out a press release. That's the scientist's version of it. Which is fine.

But if you want your story to really connect with the general public, the Logline becomes your guide map to search for the material that has effective, emotional content. For example, take an element like "taking stock" which refers to the point where the hero weighs the pros and cons of doing something.

Elements like "taking stock" which refers to the point where the hero weighs the pros and cons of doing something.

In the case of this scientist, the audience *wants* to hear the specifics about how he "took stock." They want to hear just how difficult the decision was. They *really* want to hear how he stayed up all night agonizing with his wife over whether to risk public attack and criticism by stepping out with the press release. They want to know about the arguments he had with his colleagues over this very difficult and *dramatic* decision.

And it doesn't call for him to fudge anything or be dishonest. It's just pushing for a different set of information that the analytical person might find trivial, but is what the general public (remembering what Nobel Laureate Kahneman said) connects best with. There's your basic divide at work.

If you blow right by "taking stock" and say only, "I talked to my colleagues and we decided to do it," then you've missed an entire chance to engage the audience. The material is out there. The Logline Maker can help you find it and use it.

In the end, both the ABT and the Logline have their strengths and weaknesses. A certain story might not really work as well in both. Or maybe yours makes a terrific ABT that leads effortlessly into a more complex Logline. If someone's got thirty seconds to hear your story, give 'em the ABT, but if they've got three minutes, then your Logline is ready to go.

GEN N: THE NEUROCINEMATICS GENERATION

Let me finish this chapter with an example of putting the WSP model to work with some youngsters. I was asked by the National Academy of Engineering to do a short communications training session with a dozen kids, grades 6 through 8. They were the finalists of a Disney/Broadcom Masters Competition. These were the science and engineering superstars who had been selected from several thousand kids nationally and brought to Los Angeles for a few whirlwind days as their reward, including attending the premiere of Ironman 3 and hanging out with Robert Downey, Jr. I thought I would get a day with them, but I was told it would be only two hours, and then that was cut to just an hour. What to do in such a short time? This was the where the WSP Model first crystallized.

Each student had a science fair type project for which they had been selected. The projects were, of course, amazing—developing water purification devices for isolated villages in Africa, sequencing a gene for a disease in the family of one girl—all the sorts of things that were stunning to hear from kids of the same age I was when I was busy watching "Gilligan's Island" and sneaking sips out of my parents' booze cabinet.

I began by going around the room, having each one tell the one WORD that was at the core of their project. Most of them began with an inanimate word (genetics, desalination, navigation). But with a little guidance found a more human word that captured what they were doing (empowerment, tranquility, unity). Then we moved to the one SENTENCE using the ABT template, which they picked up as if they had known it all along (even though they hadn't). And then came the most fascinating part.

I handed out the one page template/work sheet version of the Logline Maker that Dorie has developed. In our normal workshops with adults, about a third of them are at first either skeptical or confused by the Logline Maker. Pretty much everyone is a little slow to catch fire with it. We're used to this. But with these kids, it was the total opposite.

They took to the Logline Maker immediately. No explanation needed. As soon as they read, "In an ordinary world where ..." you could almost hear them say, "Oh, yeah, this—okay."

What's up with that? I'll tell you what I think is up—today's kids live their lives deeply immersed in hero movies from *Batman* to *Superman* to *Ironman* to *The Avengers*—on and on. We all had those heroes as kids in comic books, but today those heroes and their stories are being blasted at them as loudly and with as much visual stimulation as the Hollywood studios can possibly manage. And from a very early age.

Which means that their prefrontal cortices are being molded in ways my generation never could have imagined. And the result of that, I think, is that where we're all a little slow to pick up on the Logline Maker (and remember, I was skeptical of Dorie's use of it in the beginning), today's kids are like, "Oh, yeah, that thing." They are as preprogrammed to it as they are to the ABT. They are the Neurocinematics Generation.

5. THE ULTIMATE SOPHISTICATION: SIMPLICITY

Randy Olson

Time to wrap things up. So glad you were able to join us on this abbreviated journey through the practical side of storytelling. We really, really hope we've given you at least a few practical skills to develop a better real world use of the power of narrative. Here's the first note I want to leave you with.

TODAY, HOLLYWOOD IS EVERYWHERE

I opened this book telling you about my grand journey in 1993, when I packed up my entire life in New Hampshire and went to Hollywood. What I did has been a tradition in this country for an entire century.

One of my mother's best friends in junior high school in 1936 was a prime example of this. She won a beauty contest in Washington, D.C., at age 17, went to Hollywood, and grew up to be Betty Jane Greer, who costarred with Robert Mitchum in the foundational film noir movie *Out of the Past* (in 1996 we tracked her down and had a wonderfully memorable lunch with her). "Going Hollywood," has been a part of the American culture for a century.

But that tradition is now about finished. There almost isn't any Hollywood anymore because today Hollywood is everywhere. As I said at the start, in the words of Thomas Freidman, Hollywood has gone flat. The ways of thinking, the ways of talking, the short attention spans, the self-promotion, the hustling, the selling—thanks to the internet, Hollywood pretty much has become the entire American way of life.

It's similar to the premise of Dan Pink's book *To Sell Is Human*—that today we're all salespersons. I would add to it, that today we are all Hollywood.

In 1990, while I was still a professor at the University of New Hampshire, Spike Lee came and spoke (this was the night I bored the entire audience that I mentioned earlier). He was on tour after his movie *Do the Right Thing* exploded onto the American landscape. He talked about his personal mission to "demystify" filmmaking, particularly for African Americans, so they could create their own voice for their culture instead of allowing non-African Americans of Hollywood to depict them according to the perceived stereotypes. I was deeply impressed and inspired by his talk.

Well … it's a couple of decades later, and guess what, Spike, you got your wish. Today everybody is a filmmaker, which is great. Which also means that everybody is a storyteller.

So as we've said, there are thousands of years of thought and discussion behind the entire idea of "story." And yet, there's only been a world driven by Twitter and other internet hyper-charged communications resources for about five years now.

Some people like to cling to the adage, "There's nothing new under the sun," but we politely disagree. It's a different world today than from even just the 1990s—no reason to believe the same old thinking necessarily works.

AS TIME GOES BY …

It's fascinating to listen to the discussions of young Hollywood folks today (well, actually, not always fascinating, but sometimes). A viral video will erupt and you can sense a momentary feeling of, "who needs a story in this age of YouTube?" But with a little bit of examination, you begin to realize the video more than likely does indeed tell a story.

You take a closer look at the viral video and start to realize it begins with some exposition—for example, a young British boy is sitting next to his little brother, Charlie, who looks to be less than a year old and seems to have a devilish look in his eyes. But nothing has happened yet and if this is all there is then it's a "home movie" and nobody beyond their family is ever going to want to watch it.

But then the older brother puts his finger into Charlie's mouth (the *Catalytic Event!*). A look of concern sweeps over the older brother's face (*Taking Stock!*), Charlie chomps down, and a story has begun—something has happened as the older brother squeals, "Ouch!," cries a bit, followed by, "That really hurt."

The "plot" then advances a bit further as Charlie bubbles over with the sort of sadistic laugh and look in his eyes that only a little brother can know.

A few years go by and the seemingly pointless viral video of, "Charlie Bit Me" ends up with over 20 million views on You-Tube. It's not a coincidence that the basic elements of story can be seen even in a silly viral video like that, which, clearly, was not planned. Nobody sat down and charted out the three-act structure of the video in advance (but they could have!).

And yet it has a clear first act (setting up the characters, then the inciting incident), second act (older brother crying, offering commentary, Charlie producing his evil laugh), and third act (the release of tension as the brother calms down and even manages a few brief smiles to match Charlie's celebratory spirit).

If you want to test the importance of narrative structure, try taking that video and chopping it up into a different sequence of events. Have it open with the brother crying. Then the brother speaking at the start. Then Charlie smiling as the brother is crying again, but we don't know why he's crying so his smiling makes little sense. Then to a quick shot of, "Ow." And then … most people could probably put the pieces together in their mind and eventually figure out what happened, but it won't make them laugh much and it surely won't go viral. The narrative structure is the difference.

And here's further proof of storytelling not being at risk of extinction. I recently went to a USC Cinema School event and met a 25-year-old graduate who works for a "YouTube production company" in Hollywood. (He had to fill me in on what that is, as I was clueless—it's a company that makes videos for Youtube and also partners with people making popular YouTube videos, bringing in the advertising so everyone can make money.)

He told me about some of the YouTube channels they are partnered with. Their most popular channel is nothing more than a teenage kid in Sweden who makes videos of the screen of cheesy video games he's playing (he intentionally seeks the worst games) with his face in an inset box in the corner providing running commentary. I went to the channel. It's idiotic. But fun. And the guy's videos get—wait for it—170 *million* views a month.

Amazing. Most of the individual videos have about three to five million views. They're so dumb. The video games are terrible and usually from overseas with bad graphics—things like a pizza delivery boy exploring a haunted house.

So of course I began wondering if the videos themselves told much of a story. Guess what. The more they do, the more viewers they have. I found one where two guys had "green screened" themselves playing a version of Mario Brothers, where they put themselves into the game. They were on a journey. One of them got shrunk. The other was trying to help his buddy. After a while it felt like a movie. It had nine million views—the most I found. Same, same.

Storytelling is everywhere. Just think about your one comment you're going to make about this book. You're going to say, "This has been a fun book, AND I got the feeling that I was part of your workshop, BUT what I really wanted to learn about was ...; THEREFORE, would you mind ..."

That is story. That is narrative dynamics. You're using it without thinking. It's intuitive. Which leads to my final overall point.

A SENSE OF STORY

I guess I'm pretty passionate about storytelling. I opened the book by telling about how at age five I would regurgitate TV shows to my mother—like a little robot man who felt the need to consume stories then spit them back. I guarantee you that dynamic was as hard wired into my brain as neurocinematics.

And yet, I'm not that voracious of a consumer of stories. I'm definitely not obsessed with any of the standard hugely popular exercises these days in storytelling—from *Harry Potter* to *Lord of the Rings*. But I do love the scene in *Jaws* when Robert Shaw tells the story of the sinking of the *U.S.S. Indianapolis*. In fact, I worship that basic scenario—the first person, real world recounting of a journey by a real world "hero." The setting is as old as Odysseus, home from his travels. It is the essence of human culture.

In fact, one of the most hypnotic months of my entire life was the four weeks of marine biological research I conducted at the US station at McMurdo Sound, Antarctica, in the 1980s. It was long before there was an internet full of remote cameras. There were only stories.

I was there for twenty-seven days. The entire time was mind bending. I might as well have been doing crystal meth nonstop; I was so jacked up I literally slept just three to four hours a night, partly due to the twenty-four-hour daylight, but mostly due to the sheer exhilaration and feeling of "I gotta do everything—I may never get back here again!" And as if the daily adventures of diving under the ice, getting chased out of the ocean by a leopard seal, and venturing out onto the Ross Ice Shelf in blizzard conditions wasn't enough, I spent almost every evening in the dining hall listening to the Navy helicopter pilots tell their tales of near-death (for themselves) and death (for some of their comrades) around the frozen continent.

I have a weakness for that kind of storytelling. I'm part of the masses, willing and eager to be hypnotized by a great storyteller. It's wonderful. I wish we could all spin yarns like the best tellers of stories.

But we can't. Any more than we can all play in the NBA. And this, I feel is the most important thing to appreciate—that the cerebral part of storytelling, like most things in life, is not that hard. It's just like surfing, where it only took me a few weeks to read more than enough good books and articles about surfing to know the basic principles. But I've had decades of practice and am still trying to perform the basic things that I, in terms of just information, know exactly how to do.

Knowing how to do something and actually doing it—big difference.

AVOIDING "THE NERDLOOP"

Relative to this, I coined a term, "the nerdloop," a couple of years ago, addressing this. I made it up in reference to the people in the American climate movement who had done such a poor job of "telling their story" to the American public. Climate change is a heavily science-oriented issue, and the environmentalists wanting to address it bought heavily into the science side of things. Which meant they were great on the cerebral side but pretty weak on the visceral.

The problem they ran into was that to correct their poor communications (just like Obama, they failed "to tell a story to the American people") they funded more studies to gather polling data, more studies of linguistics, more studies of rhetoric—basically more semiotics ad infinitum. Which meant that rather than coming down out of their heads into the more practical, simple, real world side of communication, they just continued to get more tangled up in their endless webs of information.

And thus, the nerdloop—looping into cerebral outer space, spinning out of control in the wrong direction.

Don't be a nerdlooper. There's a reason why I partnered with two actors for our workshop rather than two professors.

We've given you the basic rules of storytelling. Now you need to set to work pursuing Gladwell's 10,000 hours of experience (or at least a few dozen) in hopes of moving everything down from your head to your gut so that you eventually do have a solid sense of story.

SIMPLICITY: THE ULTIMATE SOPHISTICATION

Now let me finish on the real importance of "story sense." It needs to be your ultimate goal. What it means is the development of story intuition. And intuition, ultimately, is everything.

I opened this book with a superlative—telling about the man who is most likely THE most important human on the planet—the President of the United States. Let me close by talking about the man who in many people's opinions was THE most important innovator of today, Steven Jobs.

Walter Isaacson wrote the definitive biography of Jobs, titled simply, *Steve Jobs*. How fitting.

In 2011, Isaacson appeared on *60 Minutes*, talking about the book. He told "the story" of the pivotal moment in Jobs professional development, which was the seven months he spent in India seeking "spiritual enlightenment." Here is what Isaacson says, which just like the Kahneman quote, is worth savoring and soaking in very deeply. He's talking about Jobs' return from India.

"And when he comes back he says the main thing I've learned is intuition—that the people of India are not just pure rational thinkers—that the great spiritual ones also have an intuition. Likewise, the simplicity of Zen Bud-

**dhism really informed his design sense—that notion that
simplicity really is the ultimate sophistication."**
  — Walter Isaacson, on *60 Minutes* 10/23/11

It's about simplicity. That's what design is about, and that's
what storytelling is about.

This is what we have pushed for with this book. Some might
find it laughable we point for a cartoon creator Trey Parker and
his three words as part of the magic to storytelling in today's
world. But we hope we've persuaded you that the important solu-
tions aren't meant to come in complicated and ornate packages.

It is through simplicity that you give your audience the ability
to retain what you've said. If you tell them a convoluted story,
they won't be able to remember it, won't be able to tell it to
friends, and ultimately the effort will be lost.

If you give them a story that, at its core, is relatively simple—
if you've managed to "crack the nut" of your material by finding out what that core theme is (ultimately, in a single word), if
you've managed to assemble it in your mind as a single sentence
using the ABT template, and if you've run it through the basic
elements of the Logline Maker to see the most powerful narrative elements in your material, then you will stand a pretty
good chance of finding the simplicity in what you want to say.
And with that simplicity, you too, will achieve "the ultimate
sophistication" as a teller of stories.

APPENDIX 1:
THE CONNECTION
STORYMAKER APP

In running our workshops we realized the WSP Model is a very effective tool for the crystallization and structuring of simple stories. This led us to create an application for smartphones and tablets that enables you to run your individual stories through the elements of the WSP Model, then save them into a library.

Figure 12. The "Splash Page" For The Connection Storymaker App.

The app is of wide value. You can use it to organize a presentation, to make an argument, to bring into focus the vision for a project—the applications of the application are limitless.

It should work well for a group as they try to achieve structure. When everyone seems confused about, "What exactly are we wanting to do here?" someone can pull out the Storymaker App and begin entering the basic elements.

The app doesn't edit your input or analyze it in any way; it just gives you the templates of the WSP Model, plus a "library" where you can save individual stories, calling them up later as you develop them.

And by the way, one little thing we've noticed … you get back from the WSP Model what you put in. If you start entering silliness, you will get back silliness and will probably think, "What a silly gimmick."

But if you think of a *real* story--one you genuinely want to work on, you'll feel a different part of your brain activating. You'll find it challenging. Compelling. When you read the finished draft, you might think, "This is good, but it could probably be even better," and you'll want to keep working on it, making it more specific, more concise, more compelling. When you hit those feelings, you'll know you're involved in real storytelling.

APPENDIX 2:
IMPROV EXERCISES

Brian Palermo

Okay, here's the fun(est) part!

I've given you the anecdotal scoop on how improv helps you become a better and more effective storyteller. Here is the experiential part. Playing the improv games yourself is active; you're out of your chair, away from your desk and hopefully out of your head (in a good way.)

So while we won't try to teach you to be funny, we do want you to use improv to improve your storytelling and thus, your reach with audiences.

There are infinite variations of improv games and exercises. You can find literally hundreds if not thousands of them online and in books. And due to the nature of the medium, anyone can create a new improv game at any time. And every school of improv has their own favorites—most are variations on similar themes. Here are a few that I find most effective. Gather some willing participants—or at least, somewhat willing—and try some of these to build your creativity and confidence, which will help your storytelling immensely.

We'll start easily. This is an acting, warm-up exercise. You don't have to be Meryl Streep, just do your best. This first step may be out of your comfort zone, and that will be a step in the right direction.

EXERCISE 1: EMOTIONAL ALPHABET

NUMBER OF PLAYERS: 2 - 15

HOW IT GOES: Group stands in a circle. Someone suggests an emotional adjustment such as any of The Big Four: Mad, Glad, Sad and Horny. One player starts and turns to the player next to him or her, makes eye contact and says the letter "A" while playing the suggested emotion. The "receiving" player then turns to the next in the circle and says "B." The group continues, sequentially, saying the letters of the alphabet, one letter at a time, with eye contact, around the circle. The players must convey the suggested emotion using facial expressions, body language, tone of voice, inflection, volume and spatial relationship to your partner (moving closer for a hug or a threat. Might be a good rule to prohibit actual touching).

However you choose to play the emotion, it must be committed to fully. For example, if the adjustment is "Happy," the players should be as happy as they can possibly be, not just slightly amused. After every round, call out a new adjustment such as Guilty, Jubilant, Shy, Afraid, Lustful, Flirtatious, Eager, Paranoid, Evil, Benevolent, etc.

WHAT IT DEVELOPS: Introduction to making and playing clear emotional choices. Builds confidence with this visceral form of expression as opposed to cerebral.

STUMBLING BLOCKS: Lack of commitment. Taking the adjustments beyond any sense of reality, being "Cartooney" as opposed to "heightened."

THE FUN ELEMENT: It's a great ice-breaker and equalizer. You may have never seen some of your partners exhibit any emotion at all much less see them fully play "Befuddled" or "Sensual."

EXERCISE 2: YES, AND...

NUMBER OF PLAYERS: 2

HOW IT GOES: Two people stand facing each other about arm's length apart. Label them Person A and Person B. Person A says one line about an event that happened to him in the past. Person B responds, starting with the words "Yes, And..." and adds a line of information that is directly related to what Person A said and moves the story forward. They continue the story back and forth. Each new sentence must begin with the words "Yes, And." A and B should play best friends who are both aware of the story being told. Having an emotional stake in the story will make it more engaging.

WHAT IT DEVELOPS:	Building creatively with another person by responding directly to what your partner has just said. Ferocious Listening skills. Giving up control.
STUMBLING BLOCKS:	Losing focus that the story is about Person A. Letting the story fall into a list of details instead of actions. Breaking eye contact.
THE FUN ELEMENT:	Seeing where the improvised story will go. Other than the very first line of dialogue, neither player has any idea where it will wind up. Getting there is all the fun.

EXAMPLE:

Person A: "Last month I went to the beach."
Person B: "Yes, and you laid out your towel."
Person A: "Yes, and I put sunscreen on."
Person B: "Yes, and you screamed and cried when you got some in your eye."

EXERCISE 3: LAST LETTER

NUMBER OF PLAYERS: 2 OR MORE

HOW IT GOES: Word tennis with a specific limitation. Someone starts by saying a word—any word. The next player must listen, determine the last letter of that word and say a new word that begins with that letter. Example: "Fracture" "Elephant" "Taco" "Ocelot" "Tremendous" "Snapdragon" etc. This can be played as a listening exercise, merely speaking words back and forth. Or it can be played as a scene, where each line of dialogue must begin with the last letter of the last word of the previous player.

WHAT IT DEVELOPS:	Listening and responding, as opposed to lecturing at people.
STUMBLING BLOCKS:	Overthinking and taking too long to respond.
THE FUN ELEMENT:	This is not a word association game, but people will often subconsciously let that element slip in. It's fun when someone responds to "Optics" with "Sexy." It's equally fun when someone responds to "Optics" with "Stupid."

Take it to another level by agreeing to play an emotional adjustment on top of the Letter game. See how your information changes when you play the game while playing Mad, Glad, Sad or Horny.

EXERCISE: IMPROVISED NOTES

I learned this one from Stanford professor, author Patricia Ryan Madson's wonderful book Improv Wisdom. Instead of writing out a speech, tell your story by answering questions— that you've asked yourself.

NUMBER OF PLAYERS: 1

HOW IT GOES: Instead of writing a talk/speech/lecture, simply write
                         down questions and answer them to the audience.

1. Who is the "hero" of my story?
2. What obstacles did she have to overcome?
3. How did she do it?
4. What changed when she was successful?

WHAT IT DEVELOPS: This technique really humanizes the speaker. Even if—
                         particularly if—there are some flubs. There is nothing
                         more natural, human and relatable than being nervous
                         speaking in front of others. So you don't have to be per-
                         fect with your presentation—only with the critical facts.
                         The rest of your story comes out as a conversation with
                         your written questions taking the place of the audience's
                         side of the interaction.

STUMBLING BLOCKS: Trying to memorize your answers, keep it loose.

THE FUN ELEMENT: I tried this exercise with my own intro speech that I do in
                         our Connection workshops and it really relaxed me. It's
                         so much more fun to have a conversation than it is to give
                         a speech.

EXERCISE 4: ONE WORD STORY

NUMBER OF PLAYERS: 2 - 15 (LIMITLESS REALLY)

HOW IT GOES: Players stand in a circle and work together to tell a story,
                         adding only one word at a time. Someone starts with a
                         short sentence with clear who, what and where in the past
                         tense. Thenthat players turns to a player on his right or
                         left, who must continue telling the story by adding only
                         the next word. Players should move the story forward
                         with step-by-step actions.

WHAT IT DEVELOPS: Focus, equal collaboration, listening, agreement.

STUMBLING BLOCKS:	Getting stuck in dialogue of what characters say instead of actions that characters do. Introducing too many characters. Over-thinking and slowing down the story.
THE FUN ELEMENT:	The one-word limit is difficult and yields stunted clarity at best. But when the players go along there can be wonderful creativity.
EXAMPLE: 1st Player:	"Jack and Jill went up the hill to get water. Jack-" Others in succession: "jumped-into-a-tree. Jill-threw-a-rope-to-him-and-climbed-up.They-ate-pickles-and-mustard-in-their-underwear. Jill-shot-Jack-a-look. Jack-climbed-out-further-into-the-leaves. A-raven-knocked-him-down."

This is an extension of the One Word Story exercise.

EXERCISE 5: ONE WORD PANEL OF EXPERTS

NUMBER OF PLAYERS: 3 PANELISTS, PLUS AN AUDIENCE OF A FEW OTHERS TO ASK QUESTIONS

HOW IT GOES:	Three people sit in chairs in front of the group and answer audience questions using a one-word-at-a-time story technique. Another player may be the moderator, or the panel can choose questions from the audience themselves. The panelists play the emotions of absolutely confident and absolutely knowledgeable. Have the audience asks questions that require a detailed answer such as "Why is the sky blue?"
	The Panel must answer this by only adding one word at a time and speaking in order until they've reached their answer's conclusion. The Panel must attack the answer with specific information, starting with any real answers they may know and improvising the rest.
WHAT IT DEVELOPS:	The ridiculous verbal constraint forces players to listen acutely and work together towards a common goal. Play-

ing emotional adjustments (fully confident and knowledgeable). Learning to build creatively.

STUMBLING BLOCKS: Players trying to control the answer, though they only
have control of one word at a time. Players taking too
long to add their next word.

THE FUN ELEMENT: These questions will invariably go awry. Even if someone—or all three of the players—knows the answer to
the question, the limitations of the game will prevent
them from getting it out in any clear way. A typical
example:

"Why is the sky blue?

"The - sky - is - blue - because - water - molecules - are -
nature's - way - of - reflecting - the - stratosphere - and - blue
- is - God's - favorite - color."

EXERCISE 6: EMOTIONAL ESCALATOR

NUMBER OF PLAYERS: 2 -15

HOW IT GOES: Everyone walks around making eye contact. One player
or the workshop leader/teacher gives them an emotional
adjustment that they all must play. The players must make
a sound or say a word/phrase that typifies the emotion.
(i.e. grief-stricken, jubilant, embarrassed.) Every time they
make eye contact with another player they must escalate
their own adjustment. As they continue, they'll ramp each
other up to a cacophony of emotional outburst.

WHAT IT DEVELOPS: Recognizing and playing emotions. Playing big. Eye
contact, awareness of others, awareness of other choices.

STUMBLING BLOCKS: Not committing to the adjustment.

THE FUN ELEMENT: This is a great warm-up exercise and a great equalizer.
Because everyone's emoting at the same time, no one
feels individually on display. It's easier to go big with an

acting adjustment when everyone else is. Played right, this
escalates to bedlam very quickly.

I got this from actor / improv teacher, David Jahn, and his
brother, Paul Jahn, who apparently works in the "real" world.
It is very brief and is more of a diagnostic tool to see how your
emotional choices are being perceived by others. Then you can
more effectively work on clarifying your emotional choices.

EXERCISE 7: IDENTIFY THE TONE

NUMBER OF PLAYERS: 2 -15

HOW IT GOES:

Players form two lines facing each other, with about 10
feet between them. The teacher whispers an emotional
adjustment, such as "confident" or "helpful," to one line
of players and they must play this adjustment as clearly as
they can, committing with their facial reactions and body
language but without words or sounds. Their partners in
the other line then observe them for 5 seconds and try to
identify the tone/emotional adjustment they are attempting to portray.

WHAT IT DEVELOPS:

An awareness that what you think you are portraying
tonally may not be how you are being perceived. Clarity
of emotional choice.

STUMBLING BLOCKS:

Don't let the players reveal their adjustment until the
partners who are trying to identify their tone have all
guessed.

THE FUN ELEMENT:

Very often when people are playing emotions that are
harder to convey than the Big Four, they are given a
shock of how they come across. It's very much like hearing your own voice when recorded; you generally don't
think you sound that way. Very fun when someone is
playing "Knowledgeable" but is perceived and labeled as
"Irritating," "Arrogant" and "Aggressive." A brilliant eye
opener.

EXERCISE 8: EMOTIONAL THREE-PEAT

NUMBER OF PLAYERS: 2 - 4

HOW IT GOES:

Get a suggestion of a type of specialty store. One person plays the clerk and the others are customers. They perform a short scene (3 or 4 lines apiece) in which a purchase gets made. The scene should be played without character or emotion. Then, they repeat the scene a couple of times word for word so they can memorize their lines. The last repetition should be a speed-through. Now they play the same scene with an emotional adjustment. The lines remain the same, but their body language, tone of voice and faces should change to reflect the adjustment. Repeat the scene a couple more times with different emotional adjustments.

WHAT IT DEVELOPS:

Shows how different emotional choices change the tone of and heighten the information/substance of the story.

STUMBLING BLOCKS:

Rushing through the lines. Not fully committing to the emotional adjustments. Players should make statements, not ask questions.

THE FUN ELEMENT:

To see the line "I need some tools to fix my garage" played angrily, then gleefully, then sensuously.

EXERCISE 9: INSTANT EXPERT

NUMBER OF PLAYERS: 1 (MORE CAN BE INVOLVED AS QUESTION-ASKERS)

HOW IT GOES:

One player starts onstage. He will act as the world's leading expert on a specific subject that the class suggests. He should immediately adopt emotional adjustments of friendly, confident and authoritative. He begins by introducing himself to the class as a character, giving his name and one or two lines about his history with the subject. Then, he answers questions from the audience by combining the knowledge he possesses with logical sounding

fabrications and a confident attitude. The speaker should
attack the question with detailed information such as
specific dates, numbers and terminology.

WHAT IT DEVELOPS: Confidence. If you can bear up under this mock pres-
sure and answer questions on any subject, imagine how
comfortable you will be delivering your actual story.

STUMBLING BLOCKS: Stalling—get right to the improvised answers. This
forces you to just let the information flow, which is much
more creative than trying to "write the answers in your
head" then share them. Vague or general information.

THE FUN ELEMENT: Watching someone answer questions about which they
have no real knowledge is a treat. I once saw a student
answer the question "How do oysters procreate?" with
a staggering amount of information that never once
touched any fact even remotely related to biology. The
upshot was basically "vodka and magic."

ACKNOWLEDGMENTS

As a group, we want to extend our deep gratitude to Jon and Gwyneth Sharp, Adrienne Sponberg and Samantha Campbell for their on-going support of our workshop, and for just being fun people who grasp the importance of telling interesting stories. Three other initial believers in us were Shelley Luce (Santa Monica Bay Restoration Foundation), Tina Swanson (Natural Resources Defense Council) and Kurt Fristrup (National Park Service), who sponsored early versions of the workshop. Each of them showed courage in supporting this project while still in the exploratory phase. Plus, we thank the workshop participants for having been fearless and courageous as Brian has made them come out of their shells through improv. Also, our good friend Joe Newman was a huge help in the crafting of this book, and Vanessa Maynard did an outstanding job with the graphic elements (book cover and interior design), plus our line editor Debra Almgren Horwitz saved us at the wire. And an extra special thanks to Josh Forgy, Jackie Yeary and Judy Barton for their helpful comments on early drafts. Now here's a few individual acknowledgments.

RANDY OLSON

I want to thank my wonderful co-authors, who have made this project the pot of gold at the end of the lengthy rainbow I've been chasing for the past three decades.

I took a lot of writing classes and even watched the Bill Moyers series with Joseph Campbell, but little of it made much sense until I began hearing it from Dorie Barton in our workshops. I have learned so much from her.

Same deal for Brian Palermo. I spent a decade working with improv actors from the Groundlings, but it wasn't until I watched Brian teach that I began to feel at least a little bit like, "I get it."

In the beginning of our workshops, I forced them both to put their ideas into fifteen-minute Powerpoint talks. For me, being a former professor, it seemed logical. But to them ... they're both actors. They had never even opened the program Powerpoint on their laptops. When they teach, they are on their feet dancing in circles, gesticulating, emoting, showing, not telling. Forcing them into the informational world of Powerpoint was like taking a couple of wild mustangs and slapping saddles on their backs. But they rose to the occasion, as they have with this book.

Furthermore, it took us a while to find the word, "Connection," as our title, but once we hit on it we found ourselves realizing over and over again it really is the perfect word for our experience—our minds truly have connected. So many people talk about the idea of bringing together scientists and artists. I've seen many projects attempting to do that, but most end up like oil and water. This has been a project where we have hybridized and blended and combined and hopefully produced a chimeric voice unlike anything previous (look that word up, Brian).

There are a whole host of other great people who made it all possible whom I already thanked in my first book (where it took three pages). All the same people are to be thanked again, with a few new additions: my enviro blogging hero Andy Revkin, my old Antarctica dive partner Ron Britton, my former co-blogger Jennifer Jacquet, my Australian marine biologist mate Lyn Devantier, my favorite munkey lover Linette, Crazy Angel and her dogs Garrett and Sedona, my hilarious neighbors at The Enchanted Sea Cottage Toni and Frank, and my yoga instructor Julie Carmen, plus an extra special smile to my wonderful mother, Muffy Moose, on her ninetieth birthday. She's been the amazing guiding light of my whole journey—the artist (a trained painter) who was able to explain to me the inherent wonderful insanity of working with artists from way back at the beginning when I transited from the relatively rational world of science to the splendid irrationality of Hollywood.

DORIE BARTON

Thanks so much to the incomparable Randy for inviting me along for this ride. A true force of nature, his generosity is matched only by his boundless enthusiasm. I feel so lucky to be included. And thanks to Brian for his humor, his brilliance, and showing us the full power of energy in action. It's wonderful to have two such terrific teammates.

None of my work in screenwriting structure would be possible without those who have blazed the trail in that field before me. The list is long, but special thanks must go to the late Blake Snyder, author of *Save the Cat*, for showing me what a joy screenwriting can be. Thanks to all my mentors over the years, especially the ones who challenged me the most. Thanks to my incredible parents for giving me an education and a curious mind; my super-smart sister, Judy, for being exactly who she is; my sweet Fisherman for teaching me patience and always showing me love; and all my amazing best friends for never—ever—getting tired of talking about stories.

BRIAN PALERMO

I wouldn't be involved with any of this splendid esoteric communications nonsense if it weren't for Randy Olson. He asked me to come play and teach and eventually, write. Thanks, dude. It's been a lot of good fun and I look forward to a lot more.Thanks also to Dorie, who has taught me so much about story. (I both love and hate that that sentence rhymes.) She is awesome.

And more than either of those two, I wish to thank my beloved wife, Michele, and my boys, Dash and Chance. They were very patient with me as I sequestered myself in our 'study' and learned whether or not I could write a (section of a) book.

Beyond them, I want to acknowledge every improviser that I ever watched, taught or played with. I learned so much and laughed so much. Theirs are the improvised shoulders on which I stand.

END NOTES

CHAPTER 1

p.   2   N. Duarte, Resonate (New York: Wiley, 2010)

p.   2   J. Gottschall, *The Storytelling Animal* (New York:
           Mariner Books, 2013)

p.   8   The Groundlings Theatre, formed in 1974, located
           at 7307 Melrose Avenue, Hollywood, California.

p.   12   Charlie Rose CBS News interview of President
           Barack Obama, June 17, 2012.

pp. 12-14 C. Vogler, *The Writer's Journey* (New York: Michael
           Weise Productions, 2007).

p.   12   Priorities USA Action, an independent expenditure
           PAC for the re-election of Barack Obama, 2012.

p.   13   J. Mayer, "Seeing Spots," *New Yorker* (November
           19, 2012) 88.36 p. 30.

p.   18   C. Kelly, "Erin Brockovich for Fascists," *Huffington
           Post*,
           December 19, 2012.

p.   27   R. Ebert, "The 11th Hour: Review," RogerEbert.
           com, August 23, 2007.

p. 29   U. Hasson, O. Landesman, B. Knappmeyer, I. Val-
         lines, N. Rubin, D. J. Heeger, *"Neurocinematics: The
         Neuroscience of Film"* Projections 2 (1): 1-26.

p. 41   HBO's *Real Sports with Bryant Gumbel*, Episode 184,
         "Gymnast Sisters," July 17, 2012.

pp. 51-52 Graff, G. and C. Birkenstein, *They Say, I Say: The
         Moves That Matter in Academia* (W.W. Norton &
         Company, 2009).

p. 51   R. McKee, Story: *Substance, Structure, Style, and the
         Principles of Screenwriting* (New York, NY: Regan-
         Books, 1997).

p. 53   D. H. Pink, *To Sell Is Human: The Surprising Truth
         About
         Moving Others* (New York, NY: Riverhead Books,
         2012).

p. 53   *Die Hard*, 1988, screenplay by Jeb Stuart, Steven E.
         de Souza.

p. 54   *6 Days to Air*, documentary aired on Comedy Cen-
         tral,
         October 9, 2011.

p. 55   M. Gladwell, *Outliers: The Story of Success*, (Boston,
         MA: Back Bay Books, 2011).

p. 61   R. Olson, "The And, But, and Therefore of Story-
         telling," presentation, TEDMED Great Challenges
         session, May 2013.

p. 63 A.B. Lord, *The Singer of Tales*, (Cambridge, MA: Harvard University Press, 2000).

p. 63 Discussion of Lord's analysis of *The Iliad* can be found in, Mills, D.H. "The Hero and the Sea: Patterns of Chaos in Ancient Myth" (Bolchazy-Carducci Publishers, 2002).

p. 76 N.D. Kristof, "Nicholas Kristof's Advice for Saving the World," *Outside magazine*, November 30, 2009.

p. 82 M. Kimmelman, "Auschwitz Shifts from Memorializing to Teaching," *New York Times*, February 18, 2011.

p. 91 *White Zombie*, was a horror film produced and directed by Victor and Edward Halperin in 1932.

p. 92 5 Second Films website, http://5secondfilms.com.

p. 95 R. Gay, "Jonah Lehrer Throws It All Away," Salon, July 31, 2012.

p. 97 *Comedian*, documentary feature film released in 2002, starring Jerry Seinfeld.

CHAPTER 2

p. 108 *Downton Abbey*: 2010, created by Julian Fellowes

p. 110 *Alien*: 1979, screenplay by Dan O'Bannon

p. 110 *Maltese Falcon*: 1941, screenplay by John Huston

p. 110 *The King's Speech*: 2010, screenplay by David Seidler

p. 116 *Homeland*: 2011, created by Howard Gordon and Alex Gansa

p. 131 *Chinatown*: 1974, Screenplay by Robert Towne

p. 133 *Flat Stanley*, 1964, is a children's book written by Jeff Brown and illustrated by Tomi Ungerer. The Flat Stanley project, started in 1995 by Dale Hubert, focuses on literacy for children by mailing paper Flat Stanley's to each other, and documenting his adventures around the world. The narrative short video, "Flat Stanley Rides a Remus", was made in 2012 by Matt Oliver, Ian Robbins, and Mark Moline.

p. 136 *Die Hard*: 1988, screenplay by Jeb Stuart & Steven E. de Souza

p. 140 *High Noon*: 1952, screenplay by Carl Foreman

p. 141 *Raiders of the Lost Ark*: 1981, screenplay by Lawrence Kasdan

p. 143 *Predator*: 1987, screenplay by Jim Thomas and Jay Thomas

p. 143 *The Proposal*: 2009, screenplay by Pete Chiarelli

p. 147 *Ocean's 11*: 1960, screenplay by Harry Brown and Charles Lederer; remake in 2001, screenplay by Ted Griffin

p. 150   *Beaches*: 1988, screenplay by Mary Agnes Donoghue

p. 152   *Harry Potter*: 2001, screenplay by Steven Kloves

p. 153   *Norma Rae*: 1979, screenplay by Irving Ravetch and Harriet Frank Jr.

p. 155   *When Harry Met Sally*: 1989, screenplay by Nora Ephron

CHAPTER 3

p. 174   K. Johnstone, *Impro: Improvisation and the Theatre (London*, UK: Faber and Faber Ltd, 1979).

pp. 177-181 P. K. Dick, *Do Androids Dream of Electric Sheep?* (New York: Random House, 1968).

p. 177   D. H. Pink, *To Sell Is Human: The Surprising Truth About Moving Others* (New York, NY: Riverhead Books, 2012).

p. 196   O. Wilde, *The Picture of Dorian Gray* (London: Penguin Classics, 2000).

p. 181   D. Goleman, *Emotional Intelligence, Why It Can Matter More Than IQ* (New York, NY: Bantam Books, 1995).

p. 181   D. Kahneman, *Thinking Fast and Slow* (New York, NY:,Farrar, Straus and Giroux, 2011).

p. 181   M. Gladwell, *Blink: The Power of Thinking Without Thinking* (New York, NY: Little, Brown and Company, 2005).

p. 182   D. Westen, *The Political Brain* (New York, NY: Public Affairs, of Perseus Books Group, 2007).

p. 191   A. Hodge, *Twentieth Century Acting Training* (New York, NY: Routledge, 2001).

p. 184   A. Mehrabian, *Silent Messages* (Belmont, CA: Wadsworth Publishing Company, 1971).

p. 189   P. Guber, "The Art of Purposeful Storytelling," *Harvard Business Review*, 2011.

CHAPTER 5

p. 237   W. Isaacson, *Steve Jobs* (New York, NY: Simon & Schuster, Inc., 2011).

INDEX